NICK MITCHELL & JONATHAN TAYLOR

UP ENCYCLOPAEDIA OF PERSONAL TRAINING

VOLUME 1

PRINCIPLES OF

MUSCLE BUILDING

PROGRAM DESIGN

A HYPERTROPHY WORKOUT MANUAL
FOR TRAINING AGES FROM
MONTHS 0 TO 24

CONTENTS

THE EXERCISE GUIDE

FOREWORD
NICK MITCHELL

NOT ANOTHER BOOK ON WEIGHT TRAINING, I HEAR YOU CRY!

The truth is that even I don't want to read, let alone write, another book on weight training. The man who has done the most to help intelligent weight training reach the widest possible audience is my friend and legendary strength coach, Charles Poliquin, and he says there's been nothing new in strength training since 1982. I couldn't agree with him more.

So what is the purpose behind this book and why is it "Volume 1"?

The books that I have written in the past, the information which I stand by and will help you get into the best shape of your life at a very rapid rate, are commercially focused "how to" manuals. They give you an all-encompassing plan, usually for 12 weeks, and the closer you follow it, the better your results will be. It's as simple as that.

They have lacked two distinct things — an explanation of "why something works" and because of that my previous books, like all "how to" manuals, fail to give the reader enough ability to adapt their programs to suit their very

IN THIS, VOLUME ONE, WE'VE GONE RIGHT BACK TO BASICS IN ORDER TO GIVE YOU THE BEST POSSIBLE FOUNDATION FROM WHICH TO PURSUE WHAT I AM EXCITED AND OPTIMISTIC TO THINK WILL BE YOUR LIFELONG LOVE AFFAIR WITH THE SINGLE BEST EXERCISE MODALITY KNOWN TO MAN — RESISTANCE TRAINING.

specific and individual needs. For a ten dollar book, you're still getting a bargain. Under no circumstances am I talking down properly done body transformation guides, but there is something lacking for those of you who want to delve a little bit deeper.

Delving deeper is what the UP Encyclopaedia Series is all about.

We want to share with you that unique combination of research, experience, and results that comes from creating the world's leading Personal Training business. A business that focuses on standards, service and results above chasing money, in the belief that having the best quality product means that commercial success will inevitably follow.

A single book cannot possibly hope to touch upon the many and varied facets of what it takes to really comprehend the art and science of optimal exercise, diet and lifestyle management. In this, volume one, we've gone right back to basics in order to give you the best possible foundation from which to pursue what I am excited and optimistic to think will be your lifelong love affair with the single best exercise modality known to man — resistance training.

The fitness industry, dominated as it is by massive gym chains and shady supplement companies, is not a great place to look at when considering the standard return on investment of the time and money that you put into it. Every commercial gym is full to the rafters with people

who have been spinning their wheels for years. For me, this is nothing less than an outright tragedy.

Whilst no one can morph into Mr. Universe in a matter of months, it is very possible, indeed unless you have health problems it should be considered downright inevitable, that you can make drastic and tangible improvements in your body composition, strength, mobility and stamina within a maximum of 12 weeks. Huge changes can be made very quickly and after that you can continue to make steady, if much slower, progress for years to come. So why does no one ever do this unless they make the mistake of falling into the anabolic steroid trap?

There are some non-negotiable elements to success that I can't give you. Commitment and persistence are essential components to getting the most from your exercise regime. However, what is abundantly clear in almost every gym in the world that I have ever visited, be it a commercial gym, a bodybuilding gym, or a personal training studio, is that very few people, including so-called professional personal trainers, have even the first clue about the key fundamentals of weight training.

As a result, this book, which just might be the most important book I am ever involved in, should be considered as a primer for everyone who lifts weights, no matter what their experience, as well as a guide for "beginners".

In this context, we also need to define what counts as a beginner because if you've had years of going to

WHILST NO ONE CAN MORPH INTO MR. UNIVERSE IN A MATTER OF MONTHS, IT IS VERY POSSIBLE, INDEED UNLESS YOU HAVE HEALTH PROBLEMS IT SHOULD BE CONSIDERED DOWNRIGHT INEVITABLE, THAT YOU CAN MAKE DRASTIC AND TANGIBLE IMPROVEMENTS IN YOUR BODY COMPOSITION, STRENGTH, MOBILITY AND STAMINA WITHIN A MAXIMUM OF 12 WEEKS.

the gym but have very little to show for it, then to me you're still a baby. What we look at is "training age", a concept that will be dealt with in greater detail in the later pages of this book – if you're one month on and one month off you've got no real training age to speak of. The programs and principles in this book are directly aimed at anyone with less than 24 months of consistent training experience.

If you've got more experience than this, is this book a waste of your time? Not at all, we all can benefit from refreshing our knowledge and what you're getting here is an insider's view into one aspect of what has helped UP to generate a ridiculous number of body transformations, all with so-called "regular people" who don't have the time to come to the gym more than three times per week. The tools that we are

about to give you will maximise your efficiency of effort to a level that would surprise even the most hyperbolic of fitness magazine covers!

In my world, what counts are results. This book, and ultimately the entire UP Encyclopaedia series, is the definitive guide to success in the gym.

SUCCESS STORIES

There's a common misconception that rapid results are just a marketing gimmick and can only be "gamed" via photo shop, fake timelines, drugs, or detraining a formerly fit person and then taking advantage of "muscle memory" to get the subject into shape in record time. Whilst all of this goes on far too much in the wider fitness industry, it doesn't happen at UP. Our clients are not aspiring fitness models or bodybuilders, they are regular people who want to maximize the efficiency of their fitness regimes.

Here's a little look at a wide selection of people who have made rapid muscular changes all whilst holding down full-time, often stressful careers and only coming into the gym three to four times a week. Never let anyone tell you that it can't be done, the power of highly focused commitment and the right training plan can work wonders!

You will note that some men have completely changed shape, whereas the women have made much more modest muscular gains. We included these to give you a range of possible outcomes that are dependent upon your own goals, genetics, persistence, and willingness to sacrifice. Please do also take into account that UP clients often experience significant body fat changes which is largely a function of diet, a subject for a later edition of the UP Encyclopaedia of Personal Training.

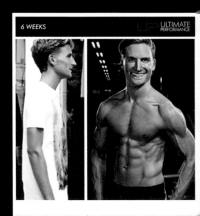

BEGINNER MUSCLE BUILDING

ARE YOU A BEGINNER?

TRAINING PROGRESSION IS A SEQUENTIAL PROCESS, WHICH MEANS THAT EVERYBODY STARTS AS A BEGINNER, BEFORE PROGRESSING TO INTERMEDIATE AND THEN ADVANCED STAGES OF DEVELOPMENT.

Nobody wants to think of themselves as a beginner, but trying to shortcut the process and start with an advanced program is the road to failure. Identifying your training age is not as straightforward as it first appears. In fact, from our work with clients, we have identified three different types of beginner, all of whom can benefit from the muscle building workouts in this book.

ALWAYS REMEMBER...

THIS ISN'T A BOOK JUST FOR BEGINNERS TO THE WORLD OF WEIGHT TRAINING.

It is a vital resource that you can refer back to throughout what I hope will be a long and lengthy love affair with the gym.

There are so many lessons to learn that no matter how good you think you are, a refresher and a reminder never go amiss. I have been at this for over thirty years myself, and as Jonathan Taylor and I have worked on the book, I've had constant small "aha!" moments that have made me want to jump into a weight rack and put the theory into practice!

TYPE **1** THE **COMPLETE BEGINNER**

TYPE **2** THE **'BORN AGAIN' BEGINNER**

TYPE **3** THE **FUNCTIONAL BEGINNER**

TYPE 1 — THE COMPLETE BEGINNER

COMPLETE BEGINNERS HAVE ZERO RESISTANCE TRAINING EXPERIENCE.

Regardless of natural strength levels, build or sporting background, anyone engaging in resistance training for the first time is a complete beginner.

Even those blessed with Arnold Schwarzenegger-style DNA must start by learning the basic skills outlined in the muscle building workouts if they are to get close to realising their full genetic potential.

TYPE 2 — THE 'BORN AGAIN' BEGINNER

BORN AGAIN BEGINNERS HAVE RESISTANCE TRAINING EXPERIENCE BUT ARE RETURNING FROM AN EXTENDED SPELL AWAY FROM TRAINING.

This is not uncommon and can happen for several reasons including competing demands on time, injury and loss of motivation.

The impact of detraining depends on:

1. The initial level of conditioning.
2. The length of absence from training.

A competitive bodybuilder who has trained intelligently for over ten years will experience a performance drop if they stop training for 12 months, but will not go all the way back to pre-training levels.

In contrast, a complete beginner who trains for 12 weeks and then stops for 12 months will lose a significant amount, if not all, of their strength and muscle gained from that 12 weeks of training.

The detraining effect is unquestionable, but it is not necessarily a case of 'use it or lose it'. The term muscle memory refers to a phenomenon in which detrained individuals experience a rapid increase in strength and muscle size upon retraining. The exact reasons why are unclear, but a combination of retained cellular machinery within muscle cells, coordination and learning all play a big part.

Despite the potential for muscle memory, anyone returning from a lengthy lay-off stands to benefit from the muscle building workouts. The main difference between them and complete beginners is that they can expect quicker progress and a shorter timeframe before they need a more advanced training program.

	Trained	Detrained
Muscle Hypertrophy	💪	💪
Maximal Strength	🏋️	🏋️
Muscular Endurance	🔋	🔋

TYPE 3 THE FUNCTIONAL BEGINNER

FUNCTIONAL BEGINNERS HAVE RESISTANCE TRAINING EXPERIENCE, BUT WITH LIMITED SUCCESS DUE TO POOR TECHNIQUE OR TRAINING STRUCTURE.

Training age is often confused with the total amount of time spent training. However, this is overly simplistic and does not consider the quality of training. You may have trained for years, but functionally remain a beginner if your technique or training structure is not very good. The one exception to this is that even the most haphazard of approaches is likely to deliver results at first. This is because someone with no resistance training experience has been exposed to so little training stress that any workout more strenuous than lying on the sofa will deliver results. **This is commonly referred to as the novice effect.**

The danger here is that the novice effect can create a false impression that a poorly designed workout is an effective one. In such situations, an initial surge in strength and muscle mass is achieved, before trainees either hit a plateau, injure themselves or get bored with a lack of results.

Your training age should be determined by an objective assessment of your progress, rather than by comparison to some external criteria. For example, some beginners with an aptitude for resistance training will bench press 100kg within six months of training, whereas this may take others one to two years despite doing everything right.

THE TRAINING AGE TEST

For anyone completely new to resistance training this will be a straightforward test.

However, for those of you already training it can be used to evaluate your approach to date.

If your level of training is more accurately described by the beginner criteria below, then you are the person we designed the muscle building workouts to help.

BEGINNER CRITERIA	INTERMEDIATE / ADVANCED CRITERIA
You do not follow a set training program or change it every week if you do.	You consistently follow a set training program for several weeks before changing.
You are prone to missing workouts when life gets busy.	You consistently train at least three times per week.
You roughly remember how you performed last week on your favourite exercise.	You record your workouts with details of sets, reps, and weight lifted.
You struggle to feel target muscle groups when performing exercises.	You have a strong 'mind-muscle' connection when performing exercises.
You have only made modest gains in muscle mass since starting training.	You have significantly more muscle mass now compared to when you started training.

GETTING STARTED

SETTING UP FOR SUCCESS

TRAINING TIMEFRAMES

PHASE 1

WK 1	⫻	⫻	⫻
WK 2	⫻	⫻	⫻
WK 3	⫻	⫻	⫻
WK 4	⫻	⫻	⫻

PHASE 2

WK 5	⫻	⫻	⫻
WK 6	⫻	⫻	⫻
WK 7	⫻	⫻	⫻
WK 8	⫻	⫻	⫻

PHASE 3

WK 9	⫻	⫻	⫻
WK 10	⫻	⫻	⫻
WK 11	⫻	⫻	⫻
WK 12	⫻	⫻	⫻

WE HAVE DESIGNED THE PROGRAM TO LAST 12 WEEKS, WHICH WE HAVE BROKEN DOWN INTO THREE 4-WEEK PHASES. THE REASON WE HAVE CHOSEN 12 WEEKS IS BECAUSE ALTHOUGH THE MUSCLE BUILDING PROCESS KICKS IN AFTER A SINGLE WORKOUT, IT CAN TAKE SEVERAL WEEKS FOR THIS TO CONVERT INTO SIGNIFICANT MUSCLE GAIN.

Compare it to renovating an old house. Builders start work on day one, but before the new house is ready, you must first demolish the old house, clear the debris, lay new foundations and only then see the new building rise up.

Expecting overnight gains in muscle mass is unrealistic, and experience shows that significant changes need at least 10 to 12 weeks of consistent resistance training.

The exact amount of time it will take you to complete the program will vary slightly based on your training frequency.

EXPECTING OVERNIGHT GAINS IN MUSCLE MASS IS UNREALISTIC, AND EXPERIENCE SHOWS THAT SIGNIFICANT CHANGES NEED AT LEAST 10 TO 12 WEEKS OF CONSISTENT RESISTANCE TRAINING.

TRAINING VOLUME AND FREQUENCY

TRAINING VOLUME IS THE TECHNICAL TERM FOR HOW MUCH WORK YOUR MUSCLES PERFORM DURING A SPECIFIC TIME PERIOD, SUCH AS A SINGLE WORKOUT OR FULL WEEK OF TRAINING.

Several factors influence training volume, including:

▶ How many exercises you include in a workout.

▶ How many sets and repetitions of each exercise you perform.

▶ How much weight you lift on each exercise.

▶ How many times you train per week.

Up to a point, there is a dose-response relationship (more = better) between training volume and muscle growth. Unsurprisingly, doing more work gets you better results. But, the point of diminishing returns exists, and increasing training volume above this can be counterproductive. Training generates fatigue and attempting to do too much can lead to overtraining.

Optimal training volume is highly individual and partly based on how much training you have previously done. The body adapts to training volume, and therefore you need to perform progressively greater amounts over time to continue making progress.

Compare it to sunbathing. At the start of summer, you only need a short period of sun exposure to start tanning. Any longer and you will burn. Over time, you will both be able and need to spend longer sunbathing to continue tanning. Similarly, somebody who has never resistance trained before will progress with a lot less training volume than an advanced trainee.

Based on this, identifying the right amount of training volume when you first start training is relatively straightforward. You need to expose your muscles to a higher level of training stress than they are used to, which is very little, while being careful not to perform so much that you struggle to recover between workouts.

One way that you can identify excessive training volumes is by the presence of a common side-effect of resistance training known as delayed onset muscle soreness (DOMS). DOMS describes pain and stiffness felt in muscles after strenuous exercise, which normally peaks at around 24 to 48 hours after a workout.

DOMS is a natural part of the training process, and it is normal for your muscles to feel sore after a workout. However, if you are still feeling sore and struggle to improve or even maintain your performance levels the next time you train that muscle group, then you have most likely overdone it!

As part of the program you will train three to four times per week, targeting each muscle group at least twice per week. It can be tempting to train more than this, but you must respect the rest days. Muscle growth does not happen during the workout itself. In fact, lifting weights breaks down and damages muscle tissue, and it is while you rest that your muscles will recover and rebuild.

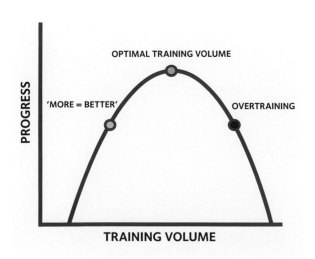

THE BEST TIME TO TRAIN

WE HAVE DIVIDED YOUR WEEKLY TRAINING INTO TWO FULL BODY WORKOUTS THAT YOU WILL ALTERNATE BETWEEN FOR A TOTAL OF THREE TO FOUR WORKOUTS PER WEEK.

When deciding the best time (day and time) to complete these workouts, you need to consider:

▶ When do you have the most energy?

▶ Competing demands on your time.

Training is important, but you need to be realistic and balance it with other commitments for it to be sustainable. Unless you are an elite athlete, your work schedule and family commitments will ultimately determine when you can or cannot train.

However, there is still some flexibility. For example, whether to train before/after work or on weekdays/weekends.

Try to avoid training on three consecutive days to give your body time to recover, although this is better than not training at all and will not affect results if you are generally on top of recovery (nutrition, sleep and stress management).

The table opposite shows two possible weekly training schedules. These are just examples and by no means the only way to organise your training.

> Each phase has two full body workouts (Workout A and Workout B), which you will alternate between until you have done each workout eight times.
>
> ---
>
> For best results, train four times per week, completing each workout twice.
>
> ---
>
> If you cannot train four times per week, aim for three and continue alternating between the workouts.

	TRAINING FREQUENCY	
	3 Workouts Per Week	**4 Workouts Per Week**
Monday	Workout A	Workout A
Tuesday	Rest Day	Workout B
Wednesday	Workout B	**Rest Day**
Thursday	Rest Day	Workout A
Friday	Workout A or B	Workout B
Saturday	Rest Day	**Rest Day**
Sunday	Rest Day	**Rest Day**

WHY FULL BODY WORKOUTS?

Full body workouts include an exercise for each of your major muscle groups (chest, back, quadriceps, glutes and hamstrings). We almost always use full body routines with new clients, as they offer several practical advantages:

- **Repetition is key to learning,** and full body workouts allow you to practice training each muscle group multiple times per week.

- **Spreading your training for a muscle group over multiple workouts,** rather than performing it all in one workout, protects the quality of your training.

- **If you can only train three times per week,** full body routines allow you to still train each muscle group more than once per week.

HOW TO INCLUDE CARDIO

THE PRIMARY ROLE OF CARDIO IN A BODY TRANSFORMATION IS TO HELP LOSE BODY FAT. THIS REQUIRES ENERGY EXPENDITURE (CALORIES BURNED) TO BE HIGHER THAN ENERGY INTAKE (CALORIES CONSUMED).

This can be achieved by performing cardio (increasing energy expenditure), caloric restriction (decreasing energy intake) or a combination of both methods.

As a result, the following recommendations are specific to people trying to lose body fat. If you are happy with your body fat levels then you do not have to (but still can) include a cardio component in your training program.

When deciding how to include cardio in your training program, it helps to distinguish between:

FORMAL CARDIO

Structured workouts deliberately performed as part of your training program. For example, treadmill running for a pre-determined amount of time.

INFORMAL CARDIO

All physical activity that is not planned exercise. Typically referred to as NEAT (non-exercise activity thermogenesis), examples include walking to work, housework and even fidgeting!

The first step is to evaluate your NEAT levels. This is difficult to do with 100% accuracy, as a large part of NEAT is subconscious, e.g. toe-tapping and fidgeting in your sleep. It is also extremely variable and affected by factors such as your nutritional status and seasonal variation.

However, we can get an accurate enough assessment based on:

▶ The amount of time you spend sitting at various time-points during the day, such as commuting to work, time spent at work and leisure time.

▶ Your daily average step total, which you can track using your mobile phone or pedometer.

The image below shows the number of steps we consider to be representative of a sedentary and active lifestyle.

ACTIVITY LEVEL	TOTAL STEPS (AVERAGE)
SEDENTARY	**< 5,000** STEPS PER DAY
LIGHTLY ACTIVE	**5,000 - 10,000** STEPS PER DAY
ACTIVE	**10,000 - 12,000** STEPS PER DAY
HIGHLY ACTIVE	**> 12,000** STEPS PER DAY

If you have low NEAT levels, our first recommendation is to aim for a daily average step target of at least 10,000 steps. The main advantage of increasing informal cardio levels first is that the low-intensity nature will not interfere with recovery from or performance in workouts.

You can then increase the rate of fat loss by introducing some type of formal cardio. The different types are identifiable based on training intensity (how hard you work) which you can measure using the following rate of perceived exertion (RPE) scale:

RATE OF PERCEIVED EXERTION (RPE) SCALE

RPE SCALE	EMOJI	WHAT THIS FEELS LIKE...
9-10	😵	**MAX EFFORT** – This pace should feel as if it is almost impossible to keep going. You will be out of breath and unable to talk.
7-8	😓	**CHALLENGING** – This pace should feel difficult to maintain and you will only be able to speak a few words.
5-6	🙁	**MODERATELY CHALLENGING** – This pace should feel uncomfortable and you will only be able to hold a short conversation.
3-4	😃	**EASY** – This pace should feel as if you can keep going for hours, while holding a full conversation.
1-2	🙂	**VERY EASY** – This pace should feel like very little effort, but more than not moving at all.

FORMAL CARDIO OPTIONS:

MODERATE INTENSITY STEADY STATE (MISS)

RPE 5-6 Moderate intensity (RPE 5-6) activity maintained for extended periods of time, e.g. 5km run.

HIGH-INTENSITY INTERVAL TRAINING (HIIT)

RPE 7-10 Alternates short periods of high-intensity exercise (RPE 7-10) with less-intense recovery periods (RPE 2-3), e.g. alternating between sprinting and walking.

The main issue to be aware of with MISS is that your body adapts specifically to the types of training that you perform. The problem this poses is that resistance training and MISS place opposite and competing demands on your body.

Resistance training conditions your muscles to lift heavy weights explosively and for short durations, whereas MISS conditions your muscles to work at lower intensities for longer durations.

This should not be an issue if you limit the amount of MISS performed, but we can avoid it altogether by using HIIT instead.

The high-intensity nature of HIIT and time spent working versus resting is very similar to resistance training, which results in complementary rather than competing adaptations.

However, there is a limit to how much training you can recover from, and both options add to the total amount of exercise-related stress placed on your body.

CARDIO RECOMMENDATIONS:

Perform the recommended cardio workout one to two times per week if training three times.

Perform the recommended cardio workout once per week if training four times.

Aim for a daily average step target of at least 10,000 steps.

These guidelines can be exceeded, and you may need to if you also have endurance-related goals, but doing so is likely to compromise your muscle building results.

Regarding timing, you should perform the cardio workouts on non-training days and never immediately before your workouts.

	3 Workouts/2 Cardio Per week	4 Workouts/1 Cardio Per week
Monday	Workout A	Workout A
Tuesday	Cardio Workout	Workout B
Wednesday	Workout B	Rest Day
Thursday	Rest Day	Workout A
Friday	Workout A or B	Workout B
Saturday	Cardio Workout	Cardio Workout
Sunday	Rest Day	Rest Day

SCHEDULING YOUR TRAINING

As part of the program, you will complete 48 workouts plus any additional cardio workouts over the course of a 12 week period. During this time, there will be many different competing demands on your time, such as:

▶ **Travel,** e.g. Holidays and business trips.

▶ **Social events,** e.g. Friends and family.

▶ **Work events,** e.g. Project deadlines.

Motivation can be fleeting and it is tempting to skip workouts when life gets busy. Identifying these situations in advance allows you to plan your training and nutrition around them proactively.

BEFORE STARTING THE PROGRAM:

STEP 1	Block off 12 weeks in your schedule.
STEP 2	Select your regular training days and times. Schedule this like you would a meeting.
STEP 3	Identify any travel, social or work-related events that might affect your regular training times.
STEP 4	Find a solution to work around these and make sure you complete the 48-workout goal.

TRAINING TIP

STRATEGICALLY PICK YOUR GYM AND TRAINING TIMES

At UP we are lucky to have access to the world's best resistance training equipment. However, working with online clients and our trainers' own experience means we are aware of the challenges that you will face when training in a commercial gym.

Every gym has busy and quiet periods, which is something you should consider when choosing your training times. This will vary across gyms, but it tends to match people's working hours, with pre–9am and post 5pm being busiest on weekdays.

The gym receptionist is the best person to speak to for advice on your gym.

It is also worth considering that the cheapest gym memberships will most likely be the busiest. Investing in a more expensive gym membership might be the best and least frustrating option, especially if you cannot be flexible with your training times.

A quick search online will reveal a list of the gyms in your local area. Treat the process like finding a new house and put aside a day to visit potential options. The last thing you want is to join a gym that does not match your needs and be locked into a contract.

THE ANATOMY OF A WORKOUT

KNOW YOUR MUSCLES

CHEST

1 Pectoralis major

2 Pectoralis minor
(beneath the pectoralis major)

SHOULDERS

3 Medial deltoid *(middle)*

4 Anterior deltoid *(front)*

5 Posterior deltoid *(back)*

ARMS

6 Biceps brachii

7 Brachialis

8 Brachioradialis

9 Triceps brachii

ABDOMINALS

10 Serratus anterior

11 Rectus abdominis

12 External obliques

13 Internal obliques
(beneath external obliques)

QUADRICEPS

14 Vastus lateralis

15 Rectus femoris

16 Vastus intermedius
(beneath rectus femoris)

17 Vastus medialis

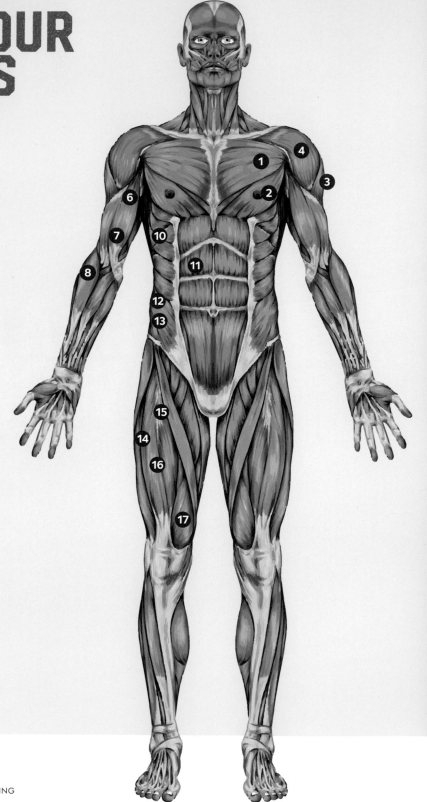

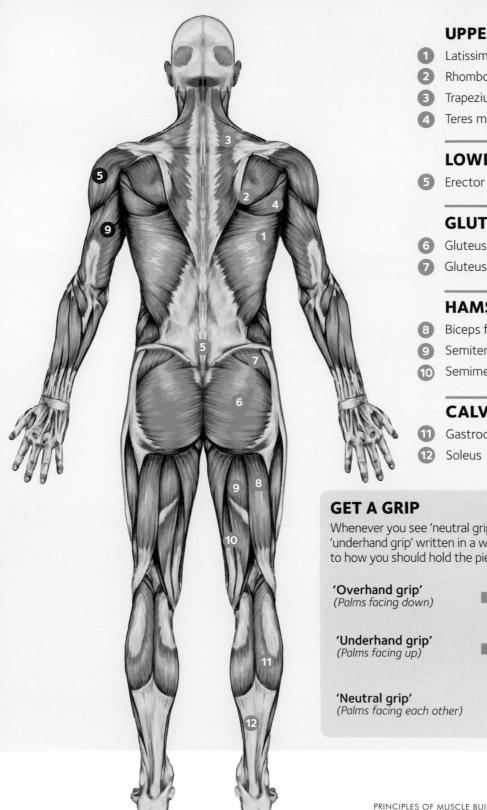

UPPER BACK

1 Latissimus dorsi
2 Rhomboid *(beneath trapezius)*
3 Trapezius
4 Teres major

LOWER BACK

5 Erector spinae muscle group

GLUTES

6 Gluteus maximus
7 Gluteus medius

HAMSTRINGS

8 Biceps femoris
9 Semitendinosus
10 Semimembranosus

CALVES

11 Gastrocnemius
12 Soleus

GET A GRIP

Whenever you see 'neutral grip', 'overhand grip', or 'underhand grip' written in a workout program it refers to how you should hold the piece of equipment.

'Overhand grip'
(Palms facing down)

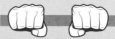

'Underhand grip'
(Palms facing up)

'Neutral grip'
(Palms facing each other)

THE ANATOMY OF A WORKOUT

① ORDER	② SETS	③ REPS	④ TEMPO	⑤ REST	⑥ DURATION
A1	3	8-10	3-0-1-0	90-120s	
A2	3	8-10	3-0-1-0	90-120s	
B1	3	8-10	3-0-1-0	90-120s	
B2	3	8-10	3-0-1-0	90-120s	60-75min *(Including warm-up)*
C1		*See Target Area Workouts*			
C2		*See Target Area Workouts*			
C3		*See Target Area Workouts*			
D	2	10-12	2-0-1-0	60-90s	

ORDER	TYPE	⑦ OPTION 1	OPTION 2	OPTION 3
A1	CHEST	30^0 Incline dumbbell press	45^0 Incline barbell press	75^0 Incline dumbbell press
A2	GLUTES AND HAMSTRINGS	Glute bridge	45^0 Incline hip extension	Barbell Romanian deadlift
B1	BACK	Neutral grip cable row	Overhand grip cable row	Single arm dumbbell row
B2	QUADS	45^0 Incline leg press	Horizontal leg press	Leg extension
C1	TARGET AREA	Chest and back	Shoulders and arms	Glutes and hamstrings
C2	TARGET AREA	Chest and back	Shoulders and arms	Glutes and hamstrings
C3	TARGET AREA	-	Shoulders and arms	-
D	ABS	Floor crunch	Exercise ball crunch	Reverse crunch

INTRO

Program design variables are the building blocks of workout programs.

Exactly how you combine these variables determines the results you get.

We have designed the workouts to:

1. Teach you the skill of resistance training.

2. Build significant amounts of muscle and strength.

1

Exercise Order and Pairings

How we structure workouts to optimise performance in each exercise.

We have placed the most demanding exercises at the start of workouts when you have the most energy.

You can perform exercises one at a time (straight sets), paired together (paired sets) or as part of a longer sequence (circuits).

2

Sets

A group of reps performed continuously without stopping.

There is a limit to how many sets you can perform before the quality of training suffers, so we must allocate the sets you do perform carefully.

3

Repetitions (Reps)

One complete movement of an exercise from start to finish. The number of reps has a big impact on weight selection and the type of adaptations made by your body in response to training.

4

Tempo (Repetition Speed)

A measure of the speed you move at during a rep. We write tempo in workout programs using a four-number sequence that breaks every rep down into four distinct phases where each number refers to the time taken (in seconds) to complete each phase.

5

Rest Period

The time dedicated to recovery between sets. How long you rest after a set has a big impact on performance in subsequent sets and how much work you can do in a fixed amount of time.

6

Workout Duration

The total time it takes to complete a workout, from warm-up to completion.

Each workout should take no longer than 60 to 75 minutes.

7

Exercise Selection

The total number and type of exercise included in a workout.

The workouts group exercises together based on the muscle groups they target.

There is no single perfect exercise and you will need to vary exercise selection over time for complete muscular development.

EXERCISE ORDER AND PAIRINGS

EXERCISE ORDER

The order of exercises in a workout can have a big impact on your performance.

Exercises differ in terms of how much weight you lift (resistance), stability, and the number of joints and muscle groups involved. This makes certain exercises more complex and fatiguing than others.

As a result, it makes sense to place the most demanding exercises at the start of workouts when you will have more energy and perform better.

As an example, the table below explains how a split squat is a more demanding exercise than a leg extension and why you would typically perform it first in a workout.

SPLIT SQUAT	LEG EXTENSION
Resistance	
Involves lifting your full bodyweight plus dumbbells.	Involves lifting the weight of your legs plus a portion of the weight-stack.
Stability	
Involves balancing on your front foot and tiptoes of your back foot.	Performed sitting down supported by a bench.
Number of muscle groups	
Targets muscle groups across your full body.	Targets your quadriceps muscles.
Number of joints	
Involves coordinating the movement of multiple joints (ankle, knee, hip), also known as a multi-joint exercise.	Movement isolated to a single joint (knee), also known as a single-joint exercise.

EXERCISE PAIRINGS

Exercises can be performed one at a time (straight sets), paired together (paired sets) or as part of a longer sequence (circuits).

STRAIGHT SETS		PAIRED SETS		CIRCUITS	
A	Flat barbell press	A1	Flat barbell press	A1	Seated dumbbell curl
		A2	Step-up	A2	Flat dumbbell triceps extension
B	Step-up			A3	Dumbbell lateral raise
		B1	Overhand grip pull-down		
C	Overhand grip pull-down	B2	Prone leg curl		

The workouts use a version of paired sets, where an upper body exercise is paired with a lower body exercise.

With paired sets, one muscle group is resting while another is working, which reduces the amount of rest you need between exercises. In comparison, straight sets are not as time efficient and require longer rest periods to maintain performance levels across multiple sets.

When pairing exercises together, it is important to consider:

Target Muscle Group Overlap

We avoid pairing exercises together that target the same muscle group. For example, pairing two chest exercises together. Although it may feel like your muscles are working harder, the fatigue generated from performing the first exercise will carry over and interfere with your performance on the second exercise. This will make it harder to maintain proper technique, you will be forced to use lighter weights and will complete fewer reps.

A better approach would be to separate the two chest exercises and either pair them with a non-competing exercise or perform them one at a time as straight sets.

Performance

If your goal was to lift the most amount of weight possible on an exercise, then we would recommend resting between sets rather than performing another exercise. However, if you are sensible with the exercises you choose to pair together, then any effect on performance should be minimal.

In fact, some people prefer paired sets and circuits as they find the longer rest periods required for straight sets boring. A common mistake many people make with straight sets is growing impatient, cutting the rest period short, and starting the next set before they have fully recovered.

Gym Logistics

Gyms can get very busy, and it will not always be possible to perform paired sets and circuits.

If this is the case, we recommend switching to straight sets, and we explain how to do so in detail in the 'How to Follow the Program' section.

NUMBER OF REPETITIONS (REPS)

HOW MANY REPS YOU CAN PERFORM DEPENDS ON THE AMOUNT OF WEIGHT YOU ARE TRYING TO LIFT. IT IS NOT ROCKET SCIENCE, THE HEAVIER OR LIGHTER A WEIGHT IS, THE FEWER OR MORE REPS ARE POSSIBLE.

Training intensity is the technical term for describing how heavy a weight is. A common way to measure training intensity is as a percentage of your one-repetition maximum (1RM). This is the heaviest weight you can lift with proper technique for one rep. So, if your bench press 1RM is 100kg then using a weight that is 80% of your 1RM would be 80kg.

We can group rep targets into the following categories:

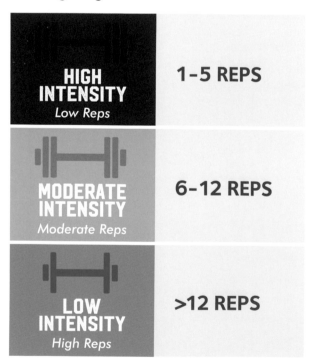

The number of reps you perform has a big impact on the adaptations made by your body in response to training.

The combination of high-intensity (heavy weights) and low reps is best for improving maximal strength, and low-intensity (light weights) and high reps are best for improving muscular endurance.

The optimal rep range for muscle growth is not as specific.

A broad range of training intensities can be effective, but the moderate rep range has several practical advantages, including:

Practice Makes Perfect

The moderate rep range gives you more practice time per set than the low rep range. However, more is not always better, and the chances of technique breakdown can increase with high rep ranges due to fatigue and loss of concentration.

Lifting Heavy Weights is a Skill

With low rep ranges, you typically expect to lift heavier weights than are possible with relatively higher rep ranges. But, this does not always play out and getting the most out of lifting heavy weights takes time and practice.

Lifting heavy weights is a skill and trying to lift and control your 1RM feels very different to a weight that you could lift for 12 reps. As a result, it is not uncommon for somebody relatively new to training to be unable to lift significantly heavier weights in the low rep range versus the moderate rep range. Attempting to do so can result in technique breakdown and injury.

You will notice that the rep ranges listed in the workouts do not change over the course of the 12 weeks. This is not us being lazy. At the start of your training career, you will benefit most from sticking to a consistent rep range. In fact, changing rep ranges too often can interrupt your progress as every time you change you will have to experiment to find the right weight.

NUMBER OF SETS

EVEN WITH THE BEST OF INTENTIONS, THERE IS A LIMIT TO HOW MUCH TRAINING YOU CAN PERFORM IN A SINGLE WORKOUT.

Mental and physical fatigue both build up over the course of a workout, and you will always reach a point where if you continue to train, you will:

▶ Struggle to main proper technique.

▶ Experience a significant drop-off in how much weight you can lift.

From experience, we know that once you factor in rest times and how long it takes to wait for equipment to become available and then set up, you can perform roughly 20 sets of 8-12 reps per 60-minute workout.

This means we have a limited number of sets to share between all the exercises we want to include in a workout.

It very rarely makes sense to only perform one set of an exercise, as this will severely restrict your practice time. When performing an exercise, you will notice aspects of your technique that you could improve. Performing multiple sets allows you to identify and correct these issues straight away, rather than having to wait until the next workout.

Research studies designed to investigate the effects of different numbers of sets on muscle growth have consistently shown that workouts including multiple sets per exercise outperform single set workout programs. As we learned earlier, doing more work gets you better results.

However, a potential problem with performing multiple sets of a single exercise is that you risk limiting how many other exercises you can perform in a workout. For example, based on the above estimate of 20 sets per workout, performing five sets per exercise would limit you to only four exercises. The problem here is that you risk neglecting certain muscle groups.

We have based the workouts on three sets per exercise, as it will allow you to refine your technique from set-to-set without overly limiting the number of exercises and muscle groups you can train during each workout.

On a related note, you may see people in your gym whose workouts seem to take hours. Do not let this fool you, as in most cases they are only training for a small percentage of this time and spend the rest of it talking to friends and playing on their mobile phones!

THERE IS A LIMIT TO HOW MUCH QUALITY WORK YOUR MUSCLES CAN PERFORM IN A SINGLE WORKOUT. STRUGGLING TO MAINTAIN TECHNIQUE OR A SIGNIFICANT DROP-OFF IN THE WEIGHTS USED ARE SIGNS THAT IT IS TIME TO GO HOME.

EXERCISE SELECTION

▶ **Primary muscle groups** are the major source of power during an exercise and should be what you feel working the most.

▶ **Secondary muscle groups** play more of a supporting role, maintaining your posture and providing extra power to help complete the movement.

Being able to identify target muscle groups and where they are on your body is incredibly important. The goal of an exercise is to target a specific muscle group, so without this knowledge, you won't be able to tell if you're performing an exercise correctly.

For every exercise included in the program, there is an exercise guide that identifies the primary and secondary muscle groups. You can then cross-reference this with the full body anatomy chart in 'Know your Muscles'.

"I CANNOT FEEL THE TARGET MUSCLE..."

IF YOU CANNOT FEEL A PRIMARY MUSCLE GROUP WHEN PERFORMING AN EXERCISE, IT IS MOST LIKELY TO BE AN ISSUE WITH YOUR TECHNIQUE.

For example, the incline hip extension should primarily target your glutes and hamstrings, but many people struggle to feel these muscles working and report only feeling their lower back muscles.

To perform this exercise correctly, you need to hinge on your hips while keeping your back straight, which requires a high level of body awareness.

It often takes us several workouts to teach new clients proper 'hip mechanics', so don't worry if you cannot feel a target muscle group straight away.

Check out the 'How to: Progress Weights' section for advice on how to troubleshoot your exercise technique.

INCLINE HIP EXTENSION

Target Muscle Groups

Primary
- Hamstrings muscle group
- Glutes (gluteus maximus)

Secondary
- Lower Back (erector spinae muscle group)

HIP JOINT

HIP JOINT

THE BEST EXERCISES FOR MUSCLE GROWTH

THE MUSCLE BUILDING WORKOUTS DO NOT INCLUDE SEVERAL OF THE EXERCISES THAT MANY PEOPLE HAVE TRADITIONALLY CONSIDERED AS BEING ESSENTIAL FOR BUILDING MUSCLE. THESE INCLUDE THE BARBELL BACK SQUAT, CONVENTIONAL DEADLIFT AND PULL-UPS.

These exercises require an advanced level of strength and coordination to execute correctly. Moreover, performing them incorrectly makes it very difficult to challenge the target muscle groups and significantly increases the risk of injury.

If your goal is to build muscle, there is no exercise that you MUST do.

For example, the pull-up may be an inappropriate starting point for a beginner aiming to develop their back muscles. Not many people have the relative strength or control to perform multiple reps with strict technique.

In comparison, the cable pull-down challenges mostly the same muscle groups, provides greater control over weight selection and the thigh pad keeps you locked in a stable position.

We have deliberately included exercises with shallower learning curves because they allow you to train hard from the onset while developing the strength and skills that you will carry over to more complex exercises in the future.

TARGET AREAS

The practice of 'spot reducing' body fat is a myth, but 'spot enhancing' a muscle group is possible and intelligent exercise selection can allow you to improve target areas.

Target areas are body parts that you think are less well developed or want to focus more on compared to others.

The first four exercises of each workout are the same for everyone and are essential to your long-term development. Taking the time to learn these movements and developing a general skill base will allow you to specialise more as you advance.

The final two to three exercises of each workout are for addressing target areas. We have made this easy by creating workouts that you can modify to focus more on:

▶ Chest and back.

▶ Posterior chain (glutes, hamstrings and back).

▶ Arms and shoulders.

EXERCISE VARIATION

A degree of variation in exercise selection is necessary, as there is no single perfect exercise for each muscle group. For complete muscular development, we must use several exercises that have complementary biomechanical properties and target muscles from different angles.

However, there is a limit to how many exercises we can include in a single workout. To account for this, we prioritise certain exercises and plan to include others in the future. This is part of a concept known as periodisation.

Program variation also has significant motivational benefits, as following the same workout for 12 weeks can be very boring!

Despite the many benefits of variation, we avoid making wholesale changes. Whenever you introduce new exercises to your training program, you must learn the technique and experiment to find the right weight. Excessive amounts of variation can result in too much time spent adapting to and learning new exercises.

REST PERIODS

HOW LONG YOU REST AFTER COMPLETING A SET DETERMINES HOW RECOVERED YOU ARE BEFORE STARTING THE NEXT SET. REST PERIODS CAN BE GROUPED INTO THE FOLLOWING CATEGORIES:

SHORT REST PERIODS	MODERATE REST PERIODS	LONG REST PERIODS
<60 SECONDS	**60-120** SECONDS	**>120** SECONDS

There is no proven physiological reason why a specific rest period length is best for muscle growth. However, there are practical implications associated with the different options:

TOO SHORT

Increased injury risk.

Impaired performance (number of reps completed).

JUST RIGHT

No major drop in performance from set-to-set.

Enough time to record the previous set in your workout journal.

TOO LONG

Time-consuming workouts.

No added benefit once recovered.

Interrupts workout 'flow'.

Short rest periods can be a high-risk strategy, especially with complex exercises involving heavy weights. Incomplete recovery can throw off coordination and control, which increases the risk of injury. It also reduces the number of reps that you can perform on subsequent sets compared to resting longer.

In contrast, long rest periods allow you to maintain performance over multiple sets better but limit how much work you can do if time limited. With rest periods, it is not a case of the longer, the better. Rather, that resting for too little time between sets can negatively affect your performance.

The muscle building workouts are based on moderate rest periods, which are a compromise between maintaining performance levels and not limiting how much work you can perform.

REP SPEED (TEMPO)

REP SPEED, ALSO KNOWN AS TEMPO, IS A MEASURE OF THE SPEED YOU MOVE AT DURING A REP.

We normally record rep speed in workout programs using a four-number code that was popularised by Charles Poliquin.

Based on this system, we can break every rep down into the four distinct phases illustrated below. Each number refers to the time taken (in seconds) to complete each phase.

ECCENTRIC	ISOMETRIC	CONCENTRIC	ISOMETRIC
MUSCLE LENGTHENS	PAUSE AT BOTTOM	MUSCLE SHORTENS	PAUSE AT TOP
3	1	1	1

Eccentric Phase

The eccentric phase is the part of the movement where you lower the weight. For example, bending your legs to squat down when performing the split squat.

Isometric Phase

The isometric phase is a pause that separates successive eccentric and concentric phases. For example, pausing at the bottom position when performing the split squat.

Concentric Phase

The concentric phase is the part of the movement where you lift (push or pull) the weight. For example, pushing through your legs to return to the start position when performing the split squat.

Isometric Phase

The isometric phase is a pause that separates successive concentric and eccentric phases. For example, pausing at the top position when performing the split squat.

A key point to make is that some exercises do not follow the *eccentric, isometric, concentric, isometric* order.

For example, most back exercises start with the concentric phase and you pull the cable attachment, free weight or machine in towards your body.

However, the system does not change to accommodate this, and the first number in the tempo sequence will always refer to the eccentric phase.

Rep Speed Recommendations

You will most likely start by moving slowly as you will have to consciously think about which body parts to move where. Over time, your technique will become more fluid, and you will be able to move relatively faster.

Once you have mastered an exercise technique, using appropriately challenging weights should prevent you from lifting super-fast. There is also no extra benefit to super-slow lifting tempos where each rep takes upwards of five seconds to complete. In fact, this can negatively affect your performance, as it will limit the amount of weight and number of reps you can complete on each set.

At UP, we place a strong emphasis on tempo when training our clients, because it is an excellent tool for teaching how to lift weights with control.

Once you have chosen an appropriate weight, your focus should be on performing reps in a controlled manner.

▶ Including a brief pause after each eccentric phase encourages you to lower the weight under control and to start the next rep with the proper technique and by engaging the right muscles.

▶ Including a brief pause after each concentric phase on pulling movements allows you to focus on contracting (squeezing) the target muscles. But, do not pause for too long here on pressing movements, for example, the split squat, as your muscles are resting in this position.

YOU WILL MOST LIKELY START BY MOVING SLOWLY AS YOU WILL HAVE TO CONSCIOUSLY THINK ABOUT WHICH BODY PARTS TO MOVE WHERE. OVER TIME, YOUR TECHNIQUE WILL BECOME MORE FLUID, AND YOU WILL BE ABLE TO MOVE RELATIVELY FASTER.

HOW TO TRAIN

HOW TO TRAIN
INTRODUCING THE 'HOW TO' GUIDES

EVEN THE MOST INTELLIGENTLY DESIGNED PROGRAM IS WORTHLESS, IF YOU DO NOT KNOW HOW TO TRAIN PROPERLY.

To help with this we have provided the following 'how to' guides:

HOW TO WARM UP

Learn about the dangers of warming up too much or too little and the exact warm-up routine we use with clients.

HOW TO SELECT THE RIGHT WEIGHT

Learn how to select the right starting weights on new exercises.

HOW TO PROGRESS WEIGHTS

Learn the system we use to evaluate a client's technique and decide both when and how to progress.

HOW TO KEEP A WORKOUT JOURNAL

Learn what data you should be tracking and paying attention to during your workouts.

For every exercise included in the muscle building workouts you will get access to:

Exercise guides that explain target muscles, equipment requirements and how to set up and perform the movement.

Demonstration videos that show how to set up and perform the movement from several different angles.

HOW TO: WARM UP

A WARM-UP INCLUDES EVERYTHING YOU DO IN THE PERIOD BETWEEN WALKING ONTO THE GYM FLOOR AND STARTING THE FIRST SET OF YOUR WORKOUT.

Performing a structured warm-up helps to reduce the risk of injury, improve exercise technique, and boost both your mental and physical performance.

This section will show you how to warm up efficiently and effectively for your workouts.

<5 MINS

TOO LITTLE

Muscles cold and sluggish.

Mentally distracted.

Increased injury risk.

5-15 MINS

JUST RIGHT

Muscles warmed up and feeling ready.

Mentally focused.

Technique refined.

>15 MINS

TOO MUCH

Muscles fatigued pre-workout.

Mentally drained.

Time-consuming workouts.

WARMING UP TOO LITTLE

If your warm up takes less than five minutes then you will miss out on many of the benefits, including:

Mental Preparation

Warm ups provide the perfect opportunity to put aside any distracting thoughts and to focus on the workout. For example, during the warm up you can set workout goals or visualise performing an exercise. There will also be times when you are not feeling on top form, but feel much better after starting to move.

Practicing Technique

Warm-ups are the perfect time to practice exercise technique without the distraction of heavy weights, but this only applies if you are paying attention. Too many people rush through their warm-up without concentrating.

Use your warm ups to get 'in the zone' and establish exercise technique to maximise the effectiveness of each session.

WARMING UP TOO MUCH

If your warm-up takes more than 15-minutes, then it is too long. Excessively long warm-ups can result in:

Starting Your Workout Fatigued

For most of the warm-up, you will not be exposing your muscles to a challenge that is sufficient to stimulate muscle growth. However, warming-up for too long, even with sub-maximal weights, cardio and stretches, can still generate fatigue that affects your performance in the actual workout.

Unnecessarily Long Workouts

Excessively long warm-ups mean that workouts take longer to complete, which can interfere with your schedule. There should be a rationale behind every part of your warm-up, other than delaying the start of the hard work!

WARMING UP JUST RIGHT

The aim is to find a sweet spot between warming up too much and too little. Following your warm up, you should feel mentally focused and physically prepared for the workout.

The warm up and workout combined should take no longer than 60 to 75 minutes.

THERE SHOULD BE A RATIONALE BEHIND EVERY PART OF YOUR WARM UP, OTHER THAN DELAYING THE START OF THE HARD WORK!

WARM UP RECOMMENDATIONS

**THE RECOMMENDED WARM-UP ROUTINE INVOLVES TWO PARTS.
THE GENERAL WARM-UP AND THE SPECIFIC WARM-UP.**

GENERAL WARM UP

The general warm-up involves light physical activity and movements that are not necessarily specific to your workout. For example, low to moderate intensity cardiovascular exercise.

The general warm-up will increase your overall body temperature and help you to mentally prepare for the workout, but has no technical carryover.

The general warm-up is especially important if you have been sedentary pre-workout. For example, if you are training first thing in the morning or after a long day sat behind a desk.

However, you can skip it if you have an active commute to the gym, such as cycling or walking.

GENERAL WARM-UP						
ORDER	RPE	SETS	TIME ON	OPTION 1	OPTION 2	OPTION 3
A	3-6	1	5 min	Exercise Bike	Brisk Walk	Cross Trainer

SPECIFIC WARM UP

The specific warm-up involves performing progressively heavier sets of the exercises you are going to be doing.

Starting light and building up gets you used to controlling heavier weights and provides your nervous system (responsible for coordinating muscle contractions) with the time it needs to hit peak performance.

We recommend a shorter warm-up for the target area exercises, as you will already have trained these muscles earlier in the workout. However, including a warm-up still allows you to practice exercise technique.

Perform the following specific warm-up for the first four exercises of each workout:

ORDER	SETS	REPS	WEIGHT	REST
SET 1	1	6-8	50% of your planned starting weight	60-90s
SET 2	1	6-8	75% of your planned starting weight	60-90s

Perform the following specific warm-up for the target area exercises:

ORDER	SETS	REPS	WEIGHT	REST
SET 1	1	6-8	50% of your planned starting weight	60-90s

KEY POINTS ON WARMING UP

1 **The warm up applies to the muscle building workouts only.** Warm up routines should be tailored to an individual's ability (experience and strength levels), their environment (climate) and the nature of the workout (types of exercises and rep ranges).

2 **Do not worry about being very precise with the percentages.** If the exact weight is not available, then select the next available weight. You might also prefer to adjust the percentages slightly. For example, performing the final warm up set closer to 90% of your planned starting weight.

3 **On certain exercises, bodyweight alone may be challenging.** In such situations, select an alternative exercise that targets the same muscle groups and use this for your first warm up set. For example, you can use the leg press to warm up for the split squat.

4 **Perform any stretching away from the workout and on the advice of an appropriately qualified professional.** Stick to their recommended stretches and do so consistently.

5 **None of the exercises included in the muscle building workouts require extreme levels of flexibility.** If you feel that you need to stretch to perform an exercise, then try an alternative exercise that targets the same muscle groups.

HOW TO: SELECT THE RIGHT WEIGHT

SELECTING THE RIGHT WEIGHT IS SOMETHING THAT MANY PEOPLE STRUGGLE WITH, BUT IS IMPORTANT AS CHOOSING THE WRONG WEIGHT CAN SERIOUSLY COMPROMISE YOUR TRAINING RESULTS.

The muscle building workouts use a combination of tools for applying resistance including your own bodyweight, free weights and machines.

This section will show you how to select the right starting weight for all the exercises included in the workouts.

BODYWEIGHT EXERCISES

Many of the exercises require you to lift a significant percentage of your bodyweight, which will be more challenging for some people than others.

This is because of differences in body composition, which is a measure of the proportion of body fat and lean body mass (LBM) in your body. A common misunderstanding is that LBM only refers to muscle, when in fact it describes everything in your body apart from body fat. So, in addition to muscle, it also includes things like organs, bones and skin. We generally express body composition in terms of percent body fat, e.g. 10% body fat.

Two people can weigh the same, but have very different body compositions.

For example, somebody who weighs 80kg with 10% body fat has a LBM of 72kg. In comparison, somebody who weighs 80kg with 30% body fat has a LBM of 56kg.

Despite weighing the same, the leaner person will most likely find it easier to perform exercises that involve lifting a large percentage of their bodyweight, such as the incline hip extension or split squat.

To put it bluntly, they have more functional weight and less 'dead weight'.

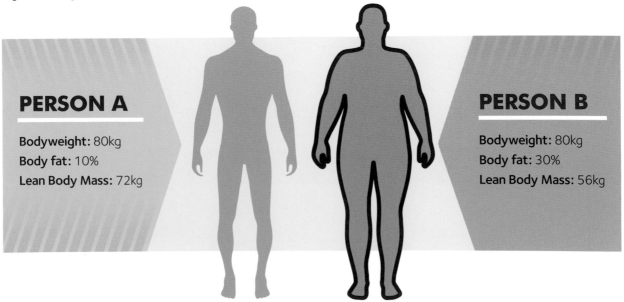

PERSON A

Bodyweight: 80kg
Body fat: 10%
Lean Body Mass: 72kg

PERSON B

Bodyweight: 80kg
Body fat: 30%
Lean Body Mass: 56kg

However, the leaner person may still struggle to learn the exercise technique. Having the keys to a Ferrari will not get you very far if you do not know how to drive!

As a result, we recommend starting with only bodyweight for resistance on some of the more complex exercises, which we have listed below.

Once you have achieved the rep target (see 'How to: Progress Weights') and are happy with your exercise technique, you can increase the challenge by progressing to using free weights.

Recommended Starting Bodyweight Exercises
▶ Floor glute bridge
▶ Hip thrust
▶ Incline hip extension
▶ Step-up
▶ Front foot flat, front foot elevated and rear foot elevated split squats
▶ Reverse lunge and walking lunge
▶ Floor crunch, exercise ball crunch and reverse crunch

FREE WEIGHT EXERCISES

Free weights are a type of exercise equipment that give you complete control over the movement path. The two main types of free weights are dumbbells and barbells.

For some exercises, only lifting your bodyweight is not challenging enough. For example, you can practice your pressing technique with only your arms for resistance to learn the movement pattern, but almost everyone can lift at least a small amount of extra weight.

In fact, this can even make it easier to learn some exercises, as it gives you something meaningful to push or pull against.

For free weight and machine exercises, the aim is to select a weight where you could perform one to three more reps than the target number with on set one. So, if you are aiming for 10 reps, you should feel like you could complete 11 to 13 on your first set.

TOO HEAVY REPS BELOW TARGET			REP TARGET	JUST RIGHT IDEAL REP RANGE			TOO LIGHT REPS ABOVE TARGET		
-3	-2	-1	0	+1	+2	+3	+4	+5	+6

For free weight and machine exercises, aim to select a weight on set one where you could perform one to three more reps than the target number with.

Not training to the point of failure on set one allows for the fact that the number of reps you can achieve on each set will reduce as your muscles fatigue. If your first set pushes you to the limit or you fail to achieve the rep target, then you are even less likely to achieve the target on the next sets.

And if you attempt to do so, you will be taking several sets close to failure, which increases the chances of technique breakdown and the risk of injury.

However, if you can complete more than three reps on set one, then the weight is too light.

The following two tables list guideline starting weights for dumbbell and barbell exercises respectively.

Differences between people in terms of build, natural strength levels and sporting background mean that you might need to do some fine-tuning. But, you should know after your first set if you have under or overestimated your strength levels and need to readjust.

 The guidelines are safe starting points and not strength standards to aim for.

GUIDELINE STARTING WEIGHTS FOR DUMBBELL EXERCISES		
Exercise	**Men**	**Women**
Dumbbell bench press	14-16kg	6-8kg
30° incline dumbbell press	14-16kg	6-8kg
75° incline dumbbell press	10-12kg	4-6kg
Dumbbell chest fly	8-10kg	3-5kg
Chest supported dumbbell row	14-16kg	8-10kg
Single-arm dumbbell row	14-16kg	8-10kg
Dumbbell biceps curl	6-8kg	3-5kg
Dumbbell preacher curl	6-8kg	3-5kg
Dumbbell triceps extension	6-8kg	3-5kg
Standing dumbbell lateral raise	3-5kg	3-5kg
Seated dumbbell lateral raise	3-5kg	3-5kg
Floor glute bridge	16-18kg	10-12kg
Hip thrust	16-18kg	10-12kg
Incline hip extension	8-10kg	4-6kg
Step-up	10-12kg	6-8kg
Split squat variations	8-10kg	4-6kg
Reverse lunge	8-10kg	4-6kg
Walking lunge	8-10kg	4-6kg
Exercise ball and floor crunch	8-10kg	4-6kg

▶ Recommendations for floor glute bridge, hip thrust, incline hip extension, exercise ball crunch and floor crunch are based on using one dumbbell.

▶ Recommendations for all other exercises are based on using a pair of dumbbells, but the weight listed is the weight of a single dumbbell and not the combined weight.

▶ Work up to using a single 20-25kg dumbbell on the floor glute bridge and hip thrust and then switch to using a barbell.

GUIDELINE STARTING WEIGHTS FOR BARBELL EXERCISES		
Exercise	**Men**	**Women**
Barbell Romanian deadlift	40-50kg	Barbell only
Floor glute bridge	40-50kg	Barbell only
Hip thrust	40-50kg	Barbell only
Barbell bench press	40-50kg	Barbell only
Incline barbell bench press	30-40kg	Barbell only

▶ Recommendations include the bar weight at 20kg.

▶ There are no universally agreed specifications for barbells, but the generic straight bars found in most gyms weigh between 15-20kg. Most gyms have weighing scales, so you can check for yourself or ask a member of staff.

▶ Make sure that you can dumbbell press more than a pair of 10kg dumbbells before attempting the barbell press.

MACHINE EXERCISES

The main difference between free weights and machines, is that the machine determines the movement path.

There are three main types:

1. Plate-loaded:
You add weight plates to the machine.

2. Weight-stack:
The weight is preloaded onto the machine, and you use a metal pin to select the weight you want to lift.

3. Cable:
Consists of a weight-stack attached via a cable and pulley system to an attachment type of your choice.

It is not uncommon for dumbbells and barbells that are supposed to weigh the same to differ slightly between gyms. However, there is a LOT more variability between different machines. For example:

1. Some weight-stacks are marked with levels, e.g. 1-20, rather than kilograms or pounds.

2. Machine design and set up can make the same weight feel more challenging on some machines than others.

3. Machine maintenance can affect how smooth the motion feels.

This makes it almost impossible to provide recommended starting weights for machine exercises. Instead, you should:

▶ Follow the instructions provided in the exercise guides to custom fit the machine to your body.

▶ Perform a set with a light weight to fine tune the setup and practice your technique.

▶ Make a conservative best guess and adjust the weight up or down on subsequent sets if necessary.

TECHNIQUE OVER EGO

Proper technique is the foundation of long-term progression. Without it, your progress will plateau, and you risk injuring yourself.

Do not worry if your starting weights are lighter than those lifted by your friends or the strongest person in the gym.

The amount of weight lifted is only one indicator of how hard your muscles are working.

It is much more challenging to lift a weight with proper technique on every rep than it is a heavier one badly.

We recommend taking a conservative approach, starting light and building up to heavier weights. This approach will build your training confidence and skills far better than being overly ambitious and having to reduce the weight and start again.

Remember, this is just a starting point and following the progression rules set out in the 'How to: Progress Weights' guide will increase your training intensity over time.

IT IS MUCH MORE CHALLENGING TO LIFT A WEIGHT WITH PROPER TECHNIQUE ON EVERY REP THAN IT IS A HEAVIER ONE BADLY.

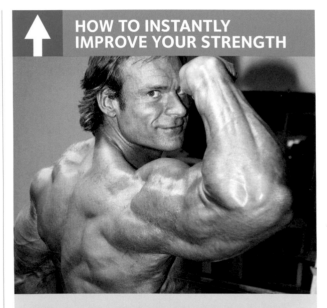

HOW TO INSTANTLY IMPROVE YOUR STRENGTH

Grip strength will always be a limiting factor and stop you from fully challenging the larger muscles of your upper and lower body.

We strongly recommend using weight lifting straps for all dumbbell, barbell and machine exercises that involve pulling or holding onto weights.

This will stop grip strength limiting how much weight you can lift and forearm fatigue distracting you during a set.

HOW TO: PROGRESS WEIGHTS

AS YOUR MUSCLES ADAPT AND BECOME STRONGER OVER TIME, YOU WILL NEED TO INCREASE THE WEIGHTS YOU ARE LIFTING TO KEEP MAKING PROGRESS.

This section will explain how to progress to lifting heavier weights as you advance through the program.

WHEN TO PROGRESS

Every exercise has a target number of sets and reps like the one below:

EXERCISE	SETS	REPS
Dumbbell bench press	3	8-10

We have written rep targets as a range, two reps wide. The goal is to achieve the higher end of the range with your selected weight.

In the example above, the goal is to complete three sets of 10 reps.

You are ready to increase the weight when:

You have achieved the upper end of the target rep-range on all sets.

Your technique is consistent from the first to the last rep.

If you fail to complete the rep target with proper technique on one or more sets, repeat the same weight until you do so (this may take more than one workout).

YOU CAN EVALUATE YOUR TECHNIQUE ON EACH SET BY ASKING YOURSELF THE FOLLOWING QUESTIONS:

☐ Did I feel the target muscle groups working?

☐ Did I feel in control of the movement at all times?

☐ Did my range of motion stay consistent?

☐ Did I feel any pain or discomfort?

You can also video record yourself performing a set, which helps to make sure that what you *think* you are doing is what you *are* doing.

'GOOD' PAIN AND 'BAD' PAIN

When reviewing your performance, you need to distinguish between 'good' training pain and 'bad' training pain.

You should expect to feel good training pain towards the end of a challenging set when your muscles are shaking with effort. However, you should only feel this in the target muscle groups, and it should subside after the set.

In comparison, bad pain can show up at any time and will feel more like a dull ache in your joints or as if your muscles are stretching too far. This can occur in non-target muscle groups and persist in some form for hours or days after the workout.

Bad pain is not a natural part of the training process, and you should not feel it if you are training with proper technique and using the right weights.

IT IS VERY IMPORTANT THAT YOU ARE HONEST WITH YOURSELF WHEN RECORDING YOUR WORKOUT. CREDITING YOURSELF WITH THE EXTRA REP PERFORMED WITH BAD TECHNIQUE MASKS PROGRESSION.

It is very important that you are honest with yourself when recording your workout. Crediting yourself with the extra rep performed with bad technique masks progression. When you eventually complete the rep with proper technique, you will not see the progress and will record a false plateau.

If you are struggling with an exercise technique or experience any pain or discomfort (other than muscular fatigue) then try:

1. Reducing the weight.

2. Switching to an alternative exercise that targets the same muscle groups.

3. Asking a personal trainer or training partner who can perform the exercise for help.

4. Make sure that you have read the accompanying exercise guide and watched the demonstration video.

HOW TO PROGRESS

To decide how to progress we use a simplified version of the rate of perceived exertion (RPE) scale developed by the professional powerlifter and coach Michael Tuchscherer and further refined by Dr Mike Zourdos, Eric Helms and their fellow researchers.

The scale is based on a concept known as repetitions in reserve (RIR), which refers to how many extra reps you can perform (if any) at the end of a set.

After the last set of every exercise ask yourself how many more reps you could have performed with proper technique:

> ▶ If you achieved the rep target, but could not complete any more reps with good technique, repeat the same weight next time.
>
> ▶ If you achieved the rep target with 1-2 RIR, increase the weight by roughly 5-10% next time.
>
> ▶ If you achieved the rep target with more than 3 RIR, increase the weight by roughly 10-15% next time.

We have written the recommendations in relative (%) terms, as seemingly small increases in weight can be suprisingly big increases. For example:

▶ Adding 5kg to 150kg deadlift is a 3% increase.

▶ Adding 1kg to a 5kg dumbbell curl is a 17% increase!

If the final set on your current weight was challenging, making too big of an increase potentially sets you on a course where your progress will soon stall.

Unfortunately, weights take up space and are expensive, so it is not uncommon for a gym's weights to increase in large steps.

If your gym is like this, you can either:

▶ **Keep the same weight and expand the rep range by one to two reps.**
For example, if you were aiming for three sets of 10 reps, the aim is now to complete three sets of 10-12 reps before dropping back down to attempt the next available weight for 10 reps.

WORKOUT	SET 1 LOAD	SET 1 REPS	SET 1 RIR	SET 2 LOAD	SET 2 REPS	SET 2 RIR	SET 3 LOAD	SET 3 REPS	SET 3 RIR
1	20kg	10	2	20kg	10	2	20kg	10	1
2	20kg	12	1	20kg	11	0	20kg	10	0
3	20kg	12	2	20kg	12	2	20kg	12	0
4	22kg	10	1	22kg	9	0	22kg	8	0

▶ **Increase the weight and reduce the rep range by one to two reps.**
For example, if you were aiming for 10 reps, the aim is now to complete three sets of six to eight reps before working back up to 10 reps with the new weight.

WORKOUT	SET 1 LOAD	SET 1 REPS	SET 1 RIR	SET 2 LOAD	SET 2 REPS	SET 2 RIR	SET 3 LOAD	SET 3 REPS	SET 3 RIR
1	20kg	10	2	20kg	10	2	20kg	10	1
2	22kg	8	1	22kg	8	0	22kg	7	0
3	22kg	8	2	22kg	8	1	22kg	8	1
4	22kg	10	0	22kg	9	0	22kg	8	0

**Do not worry if your estimates are not completely accurate to begin with.
Weight selection will always be a process of trial and error, which is why we recommend:**

1. Completing the same workout several times before changing.

2. Recording your workouts as outlined in the 'How to: Keep a Workout Journal' guide.

CHALLENGE SETS

CHALLENGE SETS ARE A TYPE OF INTENSITY TECHNIQUE THAT WE USE TO PUSH CLIENTS TO THEIR LIMITS, BUT YOU CAN ALSO USE THEM TO HELP INFORM YOUR FUTURE WEIGHT SELECTION.

The goal is to train to the point at which you cannot complete another rep with good technique. We only include challenge sets on the last set

of an exercise and explain how to do so in the 'How to Follow the Program' section.

> ⚠️ **Please note the difference between training to technical failure and training to the point at which you can no longer move your arms or legs!**

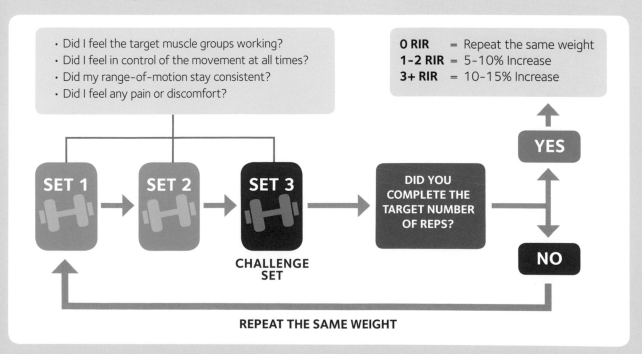

- · Did I feel the target muscle groups working?
- · Did I feel in control of the movement at all times?
- · Did my range-of-motion stay consistent?
- · Did I feel any pain or discomfort?

0 RIR	= Repeat the same weight
1–2 RIR	= 5–10% Increase
3+ RIR	= 10–15% Increase

SET 1 → **SET 2** → **SET 3**
CHALLENGE SET

DID YOU COMPLETE THE TARGET NUMBER OF REPS?

YES

NO

REPEAT THE SAME WEIGHT

Repeat the same weight on an exercise until you have completed the rep target on all sets and are happy with your technique. When you are ready to progress, you should decide how much to increase by based on the number of extra reps you managed to perform above the target number on your last set.

HOW TO: KEEP A WORKOUT JOURNAL

FOR THE BEST RESULTS, YOU MUST KEEP DETAILED RECORDS OF YOUR WORKOUTS.

You may be able to remember how much weight you lifted on your favourite exercise last week, but it is unlikely that you can recall this for every exercise in your program. It is even more unlikely that you can remember how good your technique was or how challenging you found a specific weight.

Recording your workouts can be highly motivational as it allows you to look back at the progress you have made and set goals for upcoming workouts.

This section will show you how to use a workout journal to record your workouts.

BE HONEST...

The purpose of the workout journal is to document your progress, not to impress people. Crediting yourself with the extra rep performed with dubious technique masks progression.

When you eventually complete the rep with proper technique, you will not see the progress and will record a false plateau.

HOW TO PREPARE YOUR JOURNAL

You can either record your workouts using pen and paper or keep an electronic version using your mobile phone (if you trust yourself not to get distracted!).

Before each workout, spend five to ten minutes reviewing your previous performances.

Once you have done this, you should set targets for each exercise, for example:

TARGET 1: Increase the weight

If you completed the rep target with a given weight and are happy with your technique, then you need to decide how big of an increase to make.

As discussed in the 'How to: Progress Weights' guide, you should base this decision on the number of reps you had in reserve above the target number on the last set.

You might also realise that you need to adapt the rep target if the next available weight is too big of an increase.

TARGET 2: Complete more reps with the same weight

If you failed to complete the rep target on your final set with a given weight, then you should repeat the same weight and aim for more reps.

TARGET 3: Reduce the weight

If you were overly ambitious with your weight selection or unhappy with your technique, then you should reduce the weight by an appropriate amount.

Following this, make a note of:

- ▶ Date and time.

- ▶ Extra notes on anything that may affect your performance. For example, training in a different gym or feeling under the weather.

HOW TO RECORD YOUR WORKOUT

For each workout, you will record a range of information that will provide valuable insights into your performance.

After each set, record:

▶ Amount of weight lifted.

▶ Number of sets and reps completed.

▶ Notes on difficulty. Make a note of how many additional reps you could have completed with proper technique (RIR = reps in reserve).

▶ Use the short hand descriptors listed in the 'Key' table to provide a more detailed account of your performance.

KEY	
TF	Technical failure (unhappy with technique)
INC	Increase weight next time
DEC	Decrease weight next time
REP	Repeat weight next time

	SET 1				SET 2				SET 3			
WORKOUT	**LOAD**	**REPS**	**KEY**	**RIR**	**LOAD**	**REPS**	**KEY**	**RIR**	**LOAD**	**REPS**	**KEY**	**RIR**
1	20kg	10	-	2	20kg	10	-	2	20kg	10	**TF**	2
2	20kg	10	-	1	20kg	10	-	1	20kg	10	**REP**	0
3	20kg	10	-	2	20kg	10	-	2	20kg	10	**INC**	2

In workout 1, the example trainee completed the first two sets using 20kg with good technique. However, despite performing 10 reps on the final set, they were not happy with their technique so noted 'TF'.

In workout 2, they completed 10 reps with proper technique on the final set but had no reps in reserve.

As a result, they made a note to repeat the same weight next time.

In workout 3, they again completed all three sets, but this time finished with two reps in reserve. As a result, they made a note to increase the weight next time.

THE
WORKOUTS

THE WORKOUTS
HOW TO FOLLOW THE PROGRAM

ORDER	SETS	REPS	REST	DURATION
A$_1$	3	8-10	90-120s	
A$_2$	3	8-10	90-120s	
B$_1$	3	8-10	90-120s	
B$_2$	3	8-10	90-120s	60-75min
C$_1$	*See Target Area Workouts*			
C$_2$	*See Target Area Workouts*			
C$_3$	*See Target Area Workouts*			
D	2	10-12	60-90s	

PAIRED SETS → A$_1$, A$_2$

CIRCUIT → C$_1$, C$_2$, C$_3$

STRAIGHT SET → D

WORKOUT ORDER

Straight Sets

When you see a letter without a number, e.g. A, it indicates straight sets.

- Perform one set of the exercise, e.g. A.

- Rest for the stated amount of time, e.g. 90-120 seconds.

- Repeat until you finish all the sets of that exercise and then move on to the next stage of the workout.

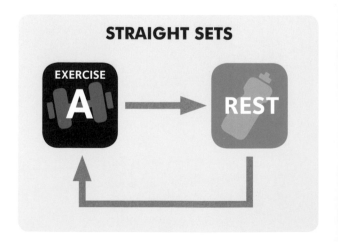

STRAIGHT SETS

EXERCISE **A** → **REST**

Paired Sets

When you see the same letter and a number in front of two exercises, e.g. A1 and A2, it indicates paired sets.

- Perform one set from the first exercise, e.g. A1.
- Rest for the stated amount of time, e.g. 90–120 seconds.
- Perform one set from the second exercise, e.g. A2.
- Rest for the stated amount of time, e.g. 90–120 seconds.
- Repeat the above steps until you finish all the sets of those exercises and then move on to the next stage of the workout.

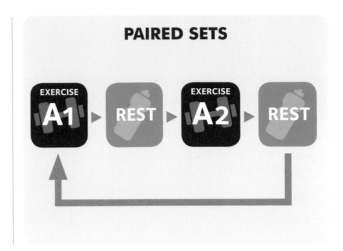

Circuits

When you see the same letter and a number in front of three exercises, e.g. A1, A2, A3, it indicates a circuit.

- Perform one set from the first exercise, e.g. A1.
- Rest for the stated amount of time, e.g. 90–120 seconds.
- Perform one set from the second exercise, e.g. A2.
- Rest for the stated amount of time, e.g. 90–120 seconds.

- Perform one set from the third exercise, e.g. A3.
- Rest for the stated amount of time, e.g. 90–120 seconds.
- Repeat the above steps until you finish all the sets of those exercises and then move on to the next stage of the workout.

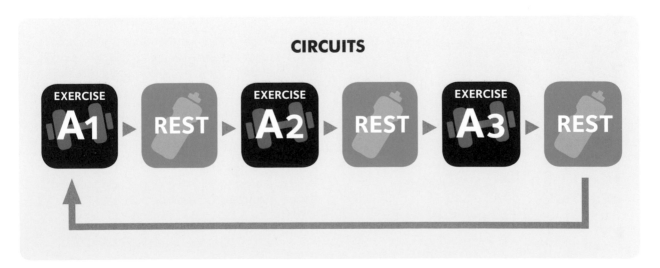

Sets, Reps and Rest Periods

Every exercise has a target number of sets and reps like the one below:

ORDER	SETS	REPS	REST
A₁	3	8-10	90-120s

We have written rep targets as a range, two reps wide. The goal is to achieve the higher end of the range with your selected weight for all sets before increasing the weight used. In the example above, the goal is to complete three sets of 10 reps.

Perform a challenge set on your last set of an exercise. To do this, simply keep on lifting until you cannot complete another rep with good exercise technique.

We have written rest periods as ranges, e.g. 60-90 seconds. Make sure to rest for the lower limit, but you can start sooner than the upper limit if you feel ready.

Tempo

The following tempo guidelines apply to all the exercises included in the program:

TEMPO GUIDELINES
PHASE: Concentric   **DURATION:** 1 second.
PHASE: Eccentric   **DURATION:** 2-3 seconds.
PHASE: Isometric (top and bottom position)   **DURATION:** 1 second.   The weight should stop moving.
TOTAL SET DURATION (8-12 REPS):   30-60 seconds.

A general guideline is that sets of 8 to 12 reps should last between 30 to 60 seconds. The exact time depends on the range of motion of the exercise. For example, you will complete 12 reps of floor crunches quicker than you will 12 reps of bench press.

If you consistently complete sets in less time, double check your technique as rushing through sets can negatively impact the quality of work.

HOW TO SELECT EXERCISES FOR PHASE 1

There are two to three exercise options to choose from for the A, B, C and D-series of each workout.

For certain exercise groupings, although the different options target the same muscle groups, some of them are more complex than others.

For example:

COMPLEX		SIMPLE
Split squat variations	▶	Step-up
Barbell Romanian deadlift	▶	Incline hip extension
Incline hip extension	▶	Floor glute bridge
Exercise ball crunch	▶	Floor crunch
20° incline reverse crunch	▶	Reverse crunch

* Refer to the individual exercise guides for more details.

We recommend starting with the simpler options in phase 1, and once you have mastered the technique, you can attempt the more complex options in later phases.

For all other exercise groupings, the different options are simply variations that target the same muscle group, but from different angles or with alternative pieces of equipment.

You can start with any option and should base your decision on equipment availability and personal preference.

HOW TO SELECT TARGET AREAS

You can modify the workouts to target certain body parts that you think are less well developed or want to focus more on compared to others.

Select a different target area for each workout from the available options:

1. Chest and back.
2. Posterior chain (glutes, hamstrings and back).
3. Arms and shoulders.

For best results, stick to the same target areas for the full 12 weeks.

You will notice some overlap between the potential exercise options for the first part of each workout (A and B-series) and the target area exercise options.

When selecting your exercises, make sure to avoid including the same exercise twice in one workout. However, you can include the same exercise in both workouts if you want extra practice or do not have access to a suitable alternative.

PHASE 1 WORKOUT

ORDER	TYPE	OPTION 1	OPTION 2	OPTION 3
A1	Chest	Dumbbell bench press (30° incline)	Dumbbell bench press (75° incline)	Barbell bench press (45° incline)
A2	Glutes + Hamstrings	Floor glute bridge	Incline hip extension (45° incline)	Barbell Romanian deadlift
B1	Back	Cable row (neutral grip)	Cable row (overhand grip)	Single arm dumbbell row
B2	Quadriceps	45° incline leg press	Horizontal leg press	Leg extension
C1	Target Area	Insert target area chest exercise	Insert target area arm exercise	Insert target area glutes/hamstring exercise
C2	Target Area	Insert target area back exercise	Insert target area arm exercise	Insert target area back exercise
C3	Target Area	–	Insert target area shoulder exercise	–
D	Abdominals	Floor crunch	Exercise ball crunch	Reverse crunch (flat or 20° incline)

PHASE 1 TARGET AREA

CHEST AND BACK						
ORDER	TYPE	OPTION 1	OPTION 2	SETS	REPS	REST
C1	Chest	Dumbbell bench press (30° incline)	Dumbbell bench press (75° incline)	3	10-12	90-120s
C2	Back	Chest supported dumbbell row	Cable row (neutral or overhand grip)	3	10-12	90-120s

SHOULDERS AND ARMS						
ORDER	TYPE	OPTION 1	OPTION 2	SETS	REPS	REST
C1	Arms	Dumbbell biceps curl (underhand grip)	Dumbbell biceps curl (neutral grip)	3	10-12	60-90s
C2	Arms	Overhead cable triceps extension	Dumbbell triceps extension	3	10-12	60-90s
C3	Shoulders	Dumbbell lateral raise (standing or seated)	Single-arm cable lateral raise	3	10-12	60-90s

POSTERIOR CHAIN						
ORDER	TYPE	OPTION 1	OPTION 2	SETS	REPS	REST
C1	Glutes + Hamstrings	Floor glute bridge	Hip thrust	3	10-12	90-120s
C2	Back	Chest supported dumbbell row	Cable row (neutral or overhand grip)	3	10-12	90-120s

HOW TO ADAPT THE WORKOUTS

Gyms can get very busy and it will not always be possible to do paired sets and circuits. If this is the case, we recommend switching to straight sets.

With straight sets, you can either:

- Alternate sets between upper body and lower body exercises.

	ORDER	EXERCISE	SETS	REPS	REST
UPPER BODY	A	Dumbbell bench press	3	8-10	120-180s
LOWER BODY	B	Floor glute bridge	3	8-10	120-180s
UPPER BODY	C	Cable row (neutral grip)	3	8-10	120-180s
LOWER BODY	D	45° incline leg press	3	8-10	120-180s

- Perform all the upper body exercises followed by the lower body exercises, or vice versa.

	ORDER	EXERCISE	SETS	REPS	REST
UPPER BODY	A	Dumbbell bench press	3	8-10	120-180s
UPPER BODY	B	Cable row (neutral grip)	3	8-10	120-180s
LOWER BODY	C	Floor glute bridge	3	8-10	120-180s
LOWER BODY	D	45° incline leg press	3	8-10	120-180s

Whichever option you choose, add roughly 50% to the rest period prescribed in the original workouts. For example, if the original workout prescribes 90-120 seconds rest, increase this to 120-180 seconds.

Make sure to rest for at least the lower limit, as not resting long enough can throw off your coordination and control, which increases the risk of injury. It will also reduce the number of reps you can complete on subsequent sets compared to resting longer.

Where possible perform paired sets, but you may have to perform the entire workout or parts of it as straight sets.

If you do have to adapt the workouts, make sure to always perform the A and B-series exercises before the C and D-series exercises.

THE WORKOUTS

PHASE

1

PHASE 1
WORKOUT

WORKOUT TABLE

ORDER	SETS	REPS	REST	DURATION
A₁	3	8-10	90-120s	
A₂	3	8-10	90-120s	
B₁	3	8-10	90-120s	
B₂	3	8-10	90-120s	60-75min
C₁		*See Target Area Workouts*		*(Including warm-up)*
C₂		*See Target Area Workouts*		
C₃		*See Target Area Workouts*		
D	2	10-12	60-90s	

EXERCISES

ORDER	TYPE	OPTION 1		OPTION 2		OPTION 3	
A₁	Chest	Dumbbell bench press (30° incline)	p. 88	Dumbbell bench press (75° incline)	p. 90	Barbell bench press (45° incline)	p. 84
A₂	Glutes + Hamstrings	Floor glute bridge	p. 126	Incline hip extension (45° incline)	p. 132	Barbell Romanian deadlift	p. 130
B₁	Back	Cable row (neutral grip)	p. 98	Cable row (overhand grip)	p. 98	Single arm dumbbell row	p. 100
B₂	Quadriceps	45° incline leg press	p. 110	Horizontal leg press	p. 112	Leg extension	p. 114
C₁	Target Area	Insert target area chest exercise		Insert target area arm exercise		Insert target area glutes/hamstrings exercise	
C₂	Target Area	Insert target area back exercise		Insert target area arm exercise		Insert target area back exercise	
C₃	Target Area	–		Insert target area shoulder exercise		–	
D	Abdominals	Floor crunch	p. 160	Exercise ball crunch	p. 162	Reverse crunch (flat or 20° incline)	p. 164

PHASE 1
WORKOUT

WORKOUT TABLE

ORDER	SETS	REPS	REST	DURATION
A$_1$	3	8-10	90-120s	
A$_2$	3	8-10	90-120s	
B$_1$	3	8-10	90-120s	
B$_2$	3	8-10	90-120s	60-75min *(Including warm-up)*
C$_1$	*See Target Area Workouts*			
C$_2$	*See Target Area Workouts*			
C$_3$	*See Target Area Workouts*			
D	2	10-12	60-90s	

EXERCISES

ORDER	TYPE	OPTION 1		OPTION 2		OPTION 3	
A$_1$	Chest	Dumbbell bench press	p. 86	Barbell bench press	p. 82	–	
A$_2$	Quadriceps	Step-up	p. 120	Split squat (front foot flat)	p. 116	Split squat (front or rear foot elevated)	p. 118
B$_1$	Back	Cable pull-down (neutral grip)	p. 102	Cable row (overhand grip)	p. 98	–	
B$_2$	Glutes + Hamstrings	Leg curl (prone)	p. 138	Leg curl (seated)	p. 138	–	
C$_1$	Target Area	Insert target area chest exercise		Insert target area arm exercise		Insert target area glutes/hamstrings exercise	
C$_2$	Target Area	Insert target area back exercise		Insert target area arm exercise		Insert target area back exercise	
C$_3$	Target Area	–		Insert target area shoulder exercise		–	
D	Abdominals	Floor crunch	p. 160	Exercise ball crunch	p. 162	Reverse crunch (flat or 20° incline)	p. 164

PHASE 1

TARGET AREA

EXERCISES

CHEST AND BACK

ORDER	TYPE	OPTION 1		OPTION 2		SETS	REPS	REST
C1	Chest	Dumbbell bench press (30° incline)	p. 88	Dumbbell bench press (75° incline)	p. 90	3	10-12	90-120s
C2	Back	Chest supported dumbbell row	p. 106	Cable row (neutral or overhand grip)	p. 98	3	10-12	90-120s

SHOULDERS AND ARMS

ORDER	TYPE	OPTION 1		OPTION 2		SETS	REPS	REST
C1	Arms	Dumbbell biceps curl (underhand grip)	p. 142	Dumbbell biceps curl (neutral grip)	p. 142	3	10-12	60-90s
C2	Arms	Overhead cable triceps extension	p. 148	Dumbbell triceps extension	p. 150	3	10-12	60-90s
C3	Shoulders	Dumbbell lateral raise (standing or seated)	p. 154	Single-arm cable lateral raise	p. 156	3	10-12	60-90s

POSTERIOR CHAIN

ORDER	TYPE	OPTION 1		OPTION 2		SETS	REPS	REST
C1	Glutes + Hamstrings	Floor glute bridge	p. 126	Hip thrust	p. 128	3	10-12	90-120s
C2	Back	Chest supported dumbbell row	p. 106	Cable row (neutral or overhand grip)	p. 98	3	10-12	90-120s

How to Change Exercises from Phase-to-Phase

At the end of each phase, look back at your weight training journal and review your performance in each exercise before selecting new ones for the next phase.

- If you are making good progress with an exercise or do not have access to an alternative option you do not have to change it. You can perform the same exercise for the full 12 weeks.

- If you are struggling with technique or dislike an exercise, you can change at this point having tried it several times.

- If you have made good progress, but like variation, then you can change and potentially return to the exercise in phase 3.

THE WORKOUTS

PHASE

2

PHASE 2
WORKOUT
A

WORKOUT TABLE

ORDER	SETS	REPS	REST	DURATION
A₁	3	8-10	90-120s	
A₂	3	8-10	90-120s	
B₁	3	8-10	90-120s	
B₂	3	8-10	90-120s	60-75min *(Including warm-up)*
C₁	*See Target Area Workouts*			
C₂	*See Target Area Workouts*			
C₃	*See Target Area Workouts*			
D	2	10-12	60-90s	

EXERCISES

ORDER	TYPE	OPTION 1		OPTION 2		OPTION 3	
A₁	Chest	Dumbbell bench press (30° incline)	p. 88	Dumbbell bench press (75° incline)	p. 90	Barbell bench press (45° incline)	p. 84
A₂	Glutes + Hamstrings	Floor glute bridge	p. 126	Incline hip extension (45° incline)	p. 132	Barbell Romanian deadlift	p. 130
B₁	Back	Cable row (neutral grip)	p. 98	Cable row (overhand grip)	p. 98	Single arm dumbbell row	p. 100
B₂	Quadriceps	45° incline leg press	p. 110	Horizontal leg press	p. 112	Leg extension	p. 114
C₁	Target Area	Insert target area chest exercise		Insert target area arm exercise		Insert target area glutes/hamstrings exercise	
C₂	Target Area	Insert target area back exercise		Insert target area arm exercise		Insert target area back exercise	
C₃	Target Area	–		Insert target area shoulder exercise		–	
D	Abdominals	Floor crunch	p. 160	Exercise ball crunch	p. 162	Reverse crunch (flat or 20° incline)	p. 164

PHASE 2
WORKOUT
B

WORKOUT TABLE

ORDER	SETS	REPS	REST	DURATION
A1	3	8-10	90-120s	
A2	3	8-10	90-120s	
B1	3	8-10	90-120s	
B2	3	8-10	90-120s	60-75min
C1	*See Target Area Workouts*			*(Including warm-up)*
C2	*See Target Area Workouts*			
C3	*See Target Area Workouts*			
D	2	10-12	60-90s	

EXERCISES

ORDER	TYPE	OPTION 1		OPTION 2		OPTION 3	
A1	Chest	Flat dumbbell bench press	p. 86	Flat barbell bench press	p. 82	–	
A2	Quadriceps	Step-up	p. 120	Split squat (front foot flat)	p. 116	Split squat (front or rear foot elevated)	p. 118
B1	Back	Cable pull-down (neutral grip)	p. 102	Cable pull-down (overhand grip)	p. 102	–	
B2	Glutes + Hamstrings	Leg curl (prone)	p. 138	Leg curl (seated)	p. 138	–	
C1	Target Area	Insert target area chest exercise		Insert target area arm exercise		Insert target area glutes/hamstrings exercise	
C2	Target Area	Insert target area back exercise		Insert target area arm exercise		Insert target area back exercise	
C3	Target Area	–		Insert target area shoulder exercise		–	
D	Abdominals	Floor crunch	p. 160	Exercise ball crunch	p. 162	Reverse crunch (flat or 20° incline)	p. 164

PHASE 2

TARGET AREA

EXERCISES

CHEST AND BACK								
ORDER	**TYPE**	**OPTION 1**		**OPTION 2**		**SETS**	**REPS**	**REST**
C1	Chest	Cable fly (standing or seated)	p. 92	Dumbbell fly	p. 94	3	10–12	90–120s
C2	Back	Straight arm cable pull-down (standing or chest supported)	p. 104	–		3	10–12	90–120s

SHOULDERS AND ARMS								
ORDER	**TYPE**	**OPTION 1**		**OPTION 2**		**SETS**	**REPS**	**REST**
C1	Arms	Dumbbell preacher curl	p. 144	Single arm preacher curl (dumbbell or cable)	p. 146	3	10–12	60–90s
C2	Arms	Cable triceps extension (standing or kneeling)	p. 152	–		3	10–12	60–90s
C3	Shoulders	Dumbbell lateral raise (standing or seated)	p. 154	Single arm cable lateral raise	p. 156	3	10–12	60–90s

POSTERIOR CHAIN								
ORDER	**TYPE**	**OPTION 1**		**OPTION 2**		**SETS**	**REPS**	**REST**
C1	Glutes + Hamstrings	Reverse lunge	p. 136	Walking lunge	p. 134	3	10–12	90–120s
C2	Back	Straight arm cable pull-down (standing or chest supported)	p. 104	–		3	10–12	90–120s

THE WORKOUTS

PHASE 3

PHASE 3
WORKOUT
A

WORKOUT TABLE

ORDER	SETS	REPS	REST	DURATION
A1	3	8-10	90-120s	
A2	3	8-10	90-120s	
B1	3	8-10	90-120s	
B2	3	8-10	90-120s	60-75min *(Including warm-up)*
C1	*See Target Area Workouts*			
C2	*See Target Area Workouts*			
C3	*See Target Area Workouts*			
D	2	10-12	60-90s	

EXERCISES

ORDER	TYPE	OPTION 1		OPTION 2		OPTION 3	
A1	Chest	Dumbbell bench press (30° incline)	p. 88	Dumbbell bench press (75° incline)	p. 90	Barbell bench press (45° incline)	p. 84
A2	Glutes + Hamstrings	Floor glute bridge	p. 126	Incline hip extension (45° incline)	p. 132	Barbell Romanian deadlift	p. 130
B1	Back	Cable row (neutral grip)	p. 98	Cable row (overhand grip)	p. 98	Single arm dumbbell row	p. 100
B2	Quadriceps	45° incline leg press	p. 110	Horizontal leg press	p. 112	Leg extension	p. 114
C1	Target Area	Insert target area chest exercise		Insert target area arm exercise		Insert target area glutes/hamstrings exercise	
C2	Target Area	Insert target area back exercise		Insert target area arm exercise		Insert target area back exercise	
C3	Target Area	–		Insert target area shoulder exercise		–	
D	Abdominals	Floor crunch	p. 160	Exercise ball crunch	p. 162	Reverse crunch (flat or 20° incline)	p. 164

PHASE 3
WORKOUT B

WORKOUT TABLE

ORDER	SETS	REPS	REST	DURATION
A1	3	8-10	90-120s	
A2	3	8-10	90-120s	
B1	3	8-10	90-120s	
B2	3	8-10	90-120s	60-75min *(Including warm-up)*
C1	See Target Area Workouts			
C2	See Target Area Workouts			
C3	See Target Area Workouts			
D	2	10-12	60-90s	

EXERCISES

ORDER	TYPE	OPTION 1		OPTION 2		OPTION 3	
A1	Chest	Flat dumbbell bench press	p. 86	Flat barbell bench press	p. 82	–	
A2	Quadriceps	Step-up	p. 120	Split squat (front foot flat)	p. 116	Split squat (front or rear foot elevated)	p. 118
B1	Back	Cable pull-down (neutral grip)	p. 102	Cable pull-down (overhand grip)	p. 102	–	
B2	Glutes + Hamstrings	Leg curl (prone)	p. 138	Leg curl (seated)	p. 138	–	
C1	Target Area	Insert target area chest exercise		Insert target area arm exercise		Insert target area glutes/hamstrings exercise	
C2	Target Area	Insert target area back exercise		Insert target area arm exercise		Insert target area back exercise	
C3	Target Area	–		Insert target area shoulder exercise		–	
D	Abdominals	Floor crunch	p. 160	Exercise ball crunch	p. 162	Reverse crunch (flat or 20° incline)	p. 164

PHASE 3

TARGET AREA

EXERCISES

CHEST AND BACK									
ORDER	**TYPE**	**OPTION 1**		**OPTION 2**		**SETS**	**REPS**	**REST**
C1	Chest	Dumbbell bench press (30° incline)	p. 88	Dumbbell bench press (75° incline)	p. 90	3	10-12	90-120s
C2	Back	Chest supported dumbbell row	p. 106	Cable row (neutral or overhand grip)	p. 98	3	10-12	90-120s

SHOULDERS AND ARMS									
ORDER	**TYPE**	**OPTION 1**		**OPTION 2**		**SETS**	**REPS**	**REST**
C1	Arms	Dumbbell biceps curl (underhand grip)	p. 142	Dumbbell biceps curl (neutral grip)	p. 142	3	10-12	60-90s
C2	Arms	Overhead cable triceps extension	p. 148	Dumbbell triceps extension	p. 150	3	10-12	60-90s
C3	Shoulders	Dumbbell lateral raise (standing or seated)	p. 154	Single arm cable lateral raise	p. 156	3	10-12	60-90s

POSTERIOR CHAIN									
ORDER	**TYPE**	**OPTION 1**		**OPTION 2**		**SETS**	**REPS**	**REST**
C1	Glutes + Hamstrings	Floor glute bridge	p. 126	Hip thrust	p. 128	3	10-12	90-120s
C2	Back	Chest supported dumbbell row	p. 106	Cable row (neutral or overhand grip)	p. 98	3	10-12	90-120s

THE WORKOUTS

CARDIO

HOW TO READ THE CARDIO PROGRAM

FOR EACH PHASE OF THE PROGRAM THERE IS AN ACCOMPANYING CARDIO WORKOUT. WE HAVE WRITTEN THESE IN LARGELY THE SAME FORMAT AS THE RESISTANCE TRAINING WORKOUTS, SO THE INSTRUCTIONS ARE VERY SIMILAR.

Workout Order

The workouts are based on straight sets and we have labelled each stage with a letter, e.g. A, B, C, D, which shows you the order to follow.

▶ Perform one set of the first exercise, e.g. A.

▶ Rest for the stated amount of time, e.g. 60-90 seconds.

▶ Repeat until you finish all the sets of that exercise and then move on to the next stage of the workout, e.g. B.

Training Intensity

The workouts alternate between high-intensity intervals where you will train as hard as possible and low-intensity exercise as recovery periods.

We use the rate of perceived exertion (RPE) scale shown below to prescribe cardio training intensity.

The intervals are based on RPE 7-10 (read, go hard!) and the recovery periods RPE 3-4 (read, go easy).

Rest Periods

We have written rest periods as ranges, e.g. 60-90 seconds, rather than fixed lengths. Make sure to rest for the lower limit, but you can start sooner than the upper limit if you feel ready.

RATE OF PERCEIVED EXERTION (RPE) SCALE		
RPE SCALE	**EMOJI**	**WHAT THIS FEELS LIKE...**
9-10	😵	**MAX EFFORT** – This pace should feel as if it is almost impossible to keep going. You will be out of breath and unable to talk.
7-8	😓	**CHALLENGING** – This pace should feel difficult to maintain and you will only be able to speak a few words.
5-6	🙁	**MODERATELY CHALLENGING** – This pace should feel uncomfortable and you will only be able to hold a short conversation.
3-4	😃	**EASY** – This pace should feel as if you can keep going for hours, while holding a full conversation.
1-2	🙂	**VERY EASY** – This pace should feel like very little effort, but more than not moving at all.

How to Select Exercises

There are three exercise options to choose from for both the low and high-intensity stages of the workout.

We have selected simple and safe options that will allow you to train hard without injuring yourself.

Sprinting is not on the list, as most people fail to ease into it and nothing stops progress like an injury!

However, you can include sprinting if you are confident in your running technique and do not have access to the other options.

Unlike with the resistance training program, you do not have to (but still can) stick to the same options for an entire phase or even the full program. In fact, varying your choices can help to keep cardio interesting.

PHASE 1

ORDER	RPE	SETS	TIME ON	TIME OFF	OPTION 1	OPTION 2	OPTION 3
A	7-10	3	20s	60-90s	Exercise bike	Rowing machine	Strongman equipment
B	3-4	1	10-15min	-	Exercise bike	Brisk walk	Cross trainer
C	7-10	1	45s	120-180s	Exercise bike	Rowing machine	Strongman equipment
D	3-4	1	10-15min	-	Exercise bike	Brisk walk	Cross trainer

PHASE 2

ORDER	RPE	SETS	TIME ON	TIME OFF	OPTION 1	OPTION 2	OPTION 3
A	7-10	4	20s	60-90s	Exercise bike	Rowing machine	Strongman equipment
B	3-4	1	10-15min	-	Exercise bike	Brisk walk	Cross trainer
C	7-10	2	45s	120-180s	Exercise bike	Rowing machine	Strongman equipment
D	3-4	1	10-15min	-	Exercise bike	Brisk walk	Cross trainer

PHASE 3

ORDER	RPE	SETS	TIME ON	TIME OFF	OPTION 1	OPTION 2	OPTION 3
A	7-10	5	20s	60-90s	Exercise bike	Rowing machine	Strongman equipment
B	3-4	1	10-15min	-	Exercise bike	Brisk walk	Cross trainer
C	7-10	3	45s	120-180s	Exercise bike	Rowing machine	Strongman equipment
D	3-4	1	10-15min	-	Exercise bike	Brisk walk	Cross trainer

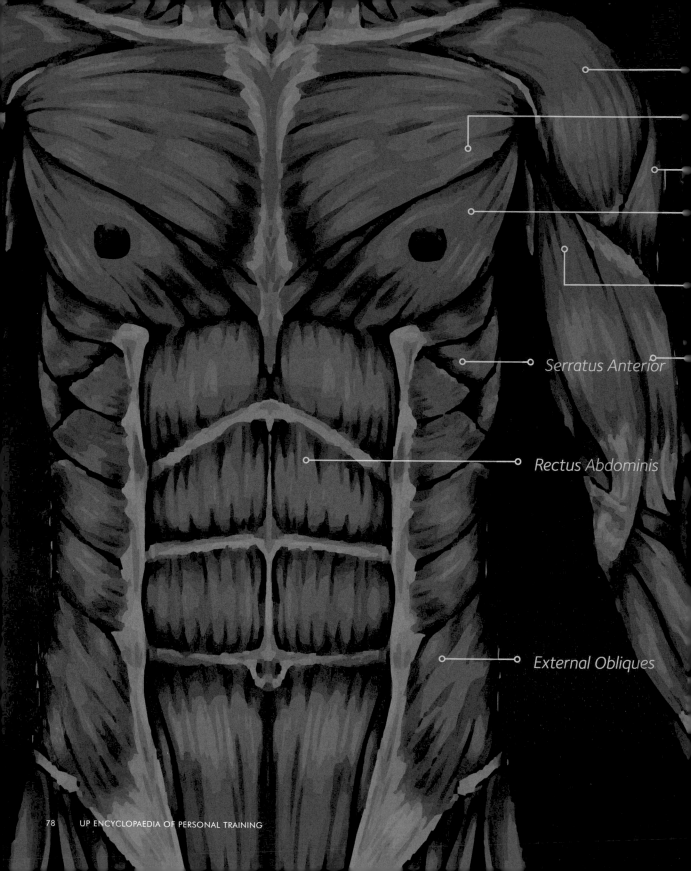

Serratus Anterior

Rectus Abdominis

External Obliques

Anterior Deltoid

Pectoralis major

Medial Deltoid

Pectoralis minor

Biceps Brachii

Brachailis

Brachioradialis

EXERCISE GUIDE

For every exercise included in the muscle building workouts, we have created a supporting guide that details:

▶ Target muscle groups.

▶ Equipment requirements.

▶ Step-by-step instructions on how to set up and perform the exercise.

▶ Pictures of the right start and finish position.

▶ Tips from UP personal trainers on how to perfect your execution.

You also get access to demonstration videos for each exercise that you can find in the video library at **www.upfitness.com**

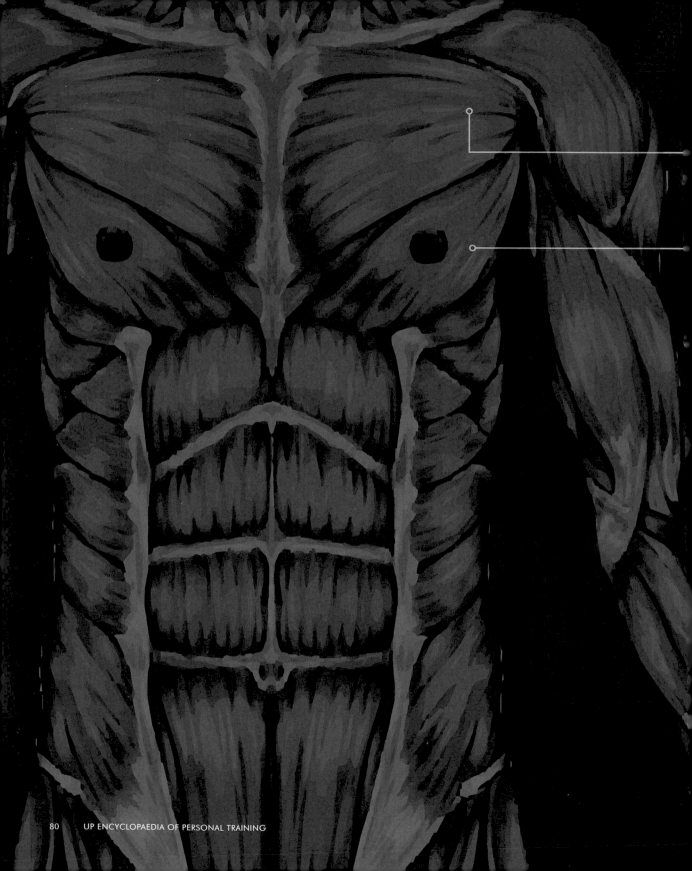

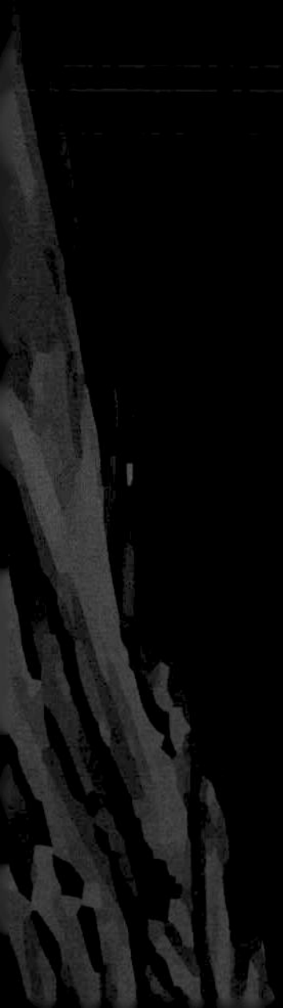

Pectoralis major

Pectoralis minor

THE EXERCISE GUIDE

CHEST

BARBELL BENCH PRESS

INCLINE BARBELL BENCH PRESS *(45º INCLINE)*

DUMBBELL BENCH PRESS

INCLINE DUMBBELL BENCH PRESS *(30º INCLINE)*

INCLINE DUMBBELL BENCH PRESS *(75º INCLINE)*

CABLE FLY *(SEATED & STANDING)*

DUMBBELL FLY

CHEST
BARBELL
BENCH PRESS

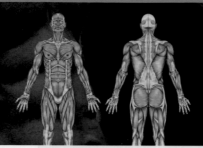

Target Muscle Groups

Primary

· Chest (pectoralis major)

Secondary

· Shoulders (anterior deltoid)
· Arms (triceps brachii)

WHAT YOU NEED:

1. Flat bench press station or power rack and flat bench.
2. Barbell.
3. Barbell collars.
4. Weight plates ranging from 1.25kg to 20kg.
5. Training partner.

NOTES:

▶ The alternative to the bench press station is the power rack, which has adjustable safety arms that you can set to catch the barbell if you fail.

▶ The bench should be wide enough to support your upper back and not so tall that you cannot keep your feet flat on the floor. Use an elevated surface, e.g. weight plates, to provide a stable base if you cannot keep your feet flat on the floor.

START

FINISH

THE SET UP

1. Position your feet shoulder-width apart, under or behind your knees and flat on the floor.

   Lie back on the bench with your eyes directly under the barbell.

2. Place your hands on the barbell with an overhand grip, roughly 1.5 times shoulder-width apart.

3. Point your chest up towards the ceiling and pinch your shoulder blades back together.

4. Your head, shoulders and glutes should be touching the bench, and there will be a small gap between your lower back and the bench.

5. Pull the barbell forwards off the hooks and into the start position directly above your shoulders.

6. Pause to let the barbell settle then fine tune your set up before starting the set.

▶ Start with a grip roughly 1.5 times shoulder-width apart and test out positions one to two inches either side to see what feels most comfortable.

▶ Do not place your feet on top of the bench. Keep them flat on the floor.

▶ Grip the barbell with your entire hand. Do not use a thumb-less grip as this increases the risk of losing control of the barbell.

▶ Pressing the barbell directly upwards off the hooks can pull your shoulder blades forwards and into an unstable position. To stop this happening, pull the barbell forwards off the hooks instead, which is much easier with the help of a training partner.

THE MOVEMENT

1. From the start position, control the barbell down towards the lower half of your chest.

2. Throughout the downward movement, your upper arms should be at an angle of 45-60° to your torso.

3. You have reached the end of your range-of-motion when you cannot lower your elbows any further below shoulder height without your chest collapsing and shoulders rotating inwards.

4. Pause for a moment before pressing the barbell upwards to return to the start position.

5. Repeat for the desired number of reps.

6. On the last rep, fully extend your arms before moving the barbell back towards the hooks.

▶ The barbell may or may not touch your chest depending on your arm length and rib cage thickness.

▶ A common mistake is for your shoulders to become loose and shrug upwards at the top of the movement. This reduces stability and shifts tension away from your chest and onto your shoulders and triceps. Focus on pushing yourself away from the barbell, instead of pressing it away from you.

▶ Be careful not to push your head back into the bench, as this can strain your neck.

CHEST
INCLINE BARBELL BENCH PRESS
(45° INCLINE)

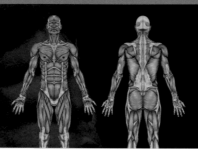

Target Muscle Groups

Primary

- Chest (pectoralis major)

Secondary

- Shoulders (anterior deltoid)
- Arms (triceps brachii)

WHAT YOU NEED:

1. Incline bench press station or power rack and adjustable bench with a 45° incline setting.

2. Barbell.

3. Barbell collars.

4. Weight plates that range from 1.25kg to 20kg.

5. Training partner.

NOTES:

▶ The alternative to the bench press station is the power rack, which has adjustable safety arms that you can set to catch the barbell if you fail.

▶ The bench should be wide enough to support your upper back and not so tall that you cannot keep your feet flat on the floor. Use an elevated surface, e.g. weight plates, to provide a stable base if you cannot keep your feet flat on the floor.

▶ Use the closest setting possible if you do not have access to a bench with a 45° incline setting.

START

FINISH

THE SET UP

1. Position your feet shoulder-width apart, under or behind your knees and flat on the floor.

2. Lie back on the bench with your eyes directly under the barbell.

3. Place your hands on the barbell with an overhand grip, roughly 1.5 times shoulder-width apart.

4. Point your chest up towards the ceiling and pinch your shoulder blades back together.

5. Your head, shoulders and glutes should be touching the bench, and there will be a small gap between your lower back and the bench.

6. Pull the barbell forwards off the hooks and into the start position directly above your shoulders.

7. Pause to let the barbell settle then fine tune your set up before starting the set.

TRAINER TIPS

- Start with a grip roughly 1.5 times shoulder-width apart and test out positions one to two inches either side to see what feels most comfortable.

- Do not place your feet on top of the bench. Keep them flat on the floor.

- Grip the barbell with your entire hand. Do not use a thumb-less grip as this increases the risk of losing control of the barbell.

- Pressing the barbell directly upwards off the hooks can pull your shoulder blades forwards and into an unstable position. To stop this happening, pull the barbell forwards off the hooks instead, which is much easier with the help of a training partner.

THE MOVEMENT

1. From the start position, control the barbell down towards the upper half of your chest.

2. Throughout the downward movement, your upper arms should be at an angle of 45-60° to your torso.

3. You have reached the end of your range-of-motion when you cannot lower your elbows any further below shoulder height without your chest collapsing and shoulders rotating inwards.

4. Pause for a moment before pressing the barbell upwards to return to the start position.

5. Repeat for the desired number of reps.

6. On the last rep, fully extend your arms before moving the barbell back towards the hooks.

TRAINER TIPS

- The set-up and movement is almost identical to the barbell bench press, but the barbell will finish in a position higher up on your chest.

- The barbell may or may not touch your chest depending on your arm length and rib cage thickness.

- A common mistake is for your shoulders to become loose and shrug upwards at the top of the movement. This reduces stability and shifts tension away from your chest and onto your shoulders and triceps. Focus on pushing yourself away from the barbell, instead of pressing it away from you.

- Be careful not to push your head back into the bench, as this can strain your neck.

CHEST
DUMBBELL
BENCH PRESS

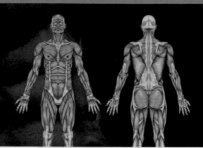

Target Muscle Groups

Primary

· Chest (pectoralis major)

Secondary

· Shoulders (anterior deltoid)
· Arms (triceps brachii)

WHAT YOU NEED:

1. Flat bench.

2. Pair of dumbbells.

NOTES:

▶ The bench should be wide enough to support your upper back and not so tall that you cannot keep your feet flat on the floor. Use an elevated surface, e.g. weight plates, to provide a stable base if you cannot keep your feet flat on the floor.

START

FINISH

THE SET UP

1. Pick up the dumbbells using a neutral grip and sit on the bench with them resting on your thighs, close to your hip crease.

2. Position your feet shoulder-width apart, under or behind your knees and flat on the floor.

3. Lie back, using your thighs to help get the dumbbells into position level with your chest.

4. Hold the dumbbells directly above your elbows, with your upper arms at an angle of 45-60° to your torso.

5. Point your chest up towards the ceiling and pinch your shoulder blades back together.

6. Your head, shoulders and glutes should be touching the bench, and there will be a small gap between your lower back and the bench.

7. This is the start and finish position for each rep.

TRAINER TIPS ★

▶ Do not place your feet on top of the bench. Keep them flat on the floor.

▶ Be very careful when manoeuvring the dumbbells in and out of position. Getting set-up to dumbbell press can be an awkward process with heavy weights, which is why we typically stick to using more moderate weights and higher reps on this exercise.

THE MOVEMENT

1. Press both dumbbells directly upwards until you have fully extended your arms overhead.

2. Reverse the motion, under control, to return to the start position.

3. You have reached the end of your range-of-motion when you cannot lower your elbows any further below shoulder height without your chest collapsing and shoulders rotating inwards.

4. Pause for a moment before repeating for the desired number of reps.

5. On the last rep, lower the dumbbells to the start position, tuck your elbows in and sit forwards using your legs to help generate momentum. Alternatively, your training partner can help by taking one dumbbell from you at a time.

TRAINER TIPS

▶ The dumbbells should not clang together at the top position.

▶ A common mistake is for your shoulders to become loose and shrug upwards at the top of the movement. This reduces stability and shifts tension away from your chest and onto your shoulders and triceps. Focus on pushing yourself away from the dumbbells, instead of pressing them away from you.

▶ Be careful not to push your head back into the bench, as this can strain your neck.

CHEST
INCLINE DUMBBELL BENCH PRESS
(30° INCLINE)

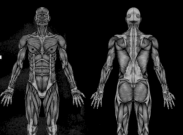

Target Muscle Groups

Primary

- Chest (pectoralis major)

Secondary

- Shoulders (anterior deltoid)
- Arms (triceps brachii)

WHAT YOU NEED:

1. Adjustable bench with a 30° incline setting.
2. Pair of dumbbells.

NOTES:

▶ The bench should be wide enough to support your upper back and not so tall that you cannot keep your feet flat on the floor. Use an elevated surface, e.g. weight plates, to provide a stable base if you cannot keep your feet flat on the floor.

▶ Use the closest setting possible if you do not have access to a bench with a 30° incline setting.

START

FINISH

THE SET UP

1. Pick up the dumbbells using a neutral grip and sit on the bench with them resting on your thighs, close to your hip crease.

2. Position your feet shoulder-width apart, under or behind your knees and flat on the floor.

3. Lie back, using your thighs to help get the dumbbells into position level with your chest.

4. Hold the dumbbells directly above your elbows, with your upper arms at an angle of 45-60° to your torso.

5. Point your chest up towards the ceiling and pinch your shoulder blades back together.

6. Your head, shoulders and glutes should be touching the bench, and there will be a small gap between your lower back and the bench.

7. This is the start and finish position for each rep.

TRAINER TIPS

▶ Do not place your feet on top of the bench. Keep them flat on the floor.

▶ Be very careful when manoeuvring the dumbbells in and out of position. Getting set-up to dumbbell press can be an awkward process with heavy weights, which is why we typically stick to using more moderate weights and higher reps on this exercise.

THE MOVEMENT

1. Press both dumbbells directly upwards until you have fully extended your arms overhead.

2. Reverse the motion, under control, to return to the start position.

3. You have reached the end of your range-of-motion when you cannot lower your elbows any further below shoulder height without your chest collapsing and shoulders rotating inwards.

4. Pause for a moment before repeating for the desired number of reps.

5. On the last rep, lower the dumbbells to the start position, tuck your elbows in and sit forwards using your legs to help generate momentum. Alternatively, your training partner can help by taking one dumbbell from you at a time.

TRAINER TIPS

▶ The set-up and movement are the same as other versions of the dumbbell bench press but this angle places more emphasis on your upper chest.

▶ The dumbbells should not clang together at the top position.

▶ A common mistake is for your shoulders to become loose and shrug upwards at the top of the movement. This reduces stability and shifts tension away from your chest and onto your shoulders and triceps. Focus on pushing yourself away from the dumbbells, instead of pressing them away from you.

▶ Be careful not to push your head back into the bench, as this can strain your neck.

CHEST
INCLINE DUMBBELL BENCH PRESS
(75° INCLINE)

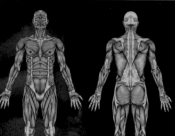

Target Muscle Groups

Primary
- Chest (pectoralis major)
- Shoulders (anterior deltoid)

Secondary
- Arms (triceps brachii)

WHAT YOU NEED:

1. Adjustable bench with a 75° incline setting.
2. Pair of dumbbells.

NOTES:

▶ The bench should be wide enough to support your upper back and not so tall that you cannot keep your feet flat on the floor. Use an elevated surface, e.g. weight plates, to provide a stable base if you cannot keep your feet flat on the floor.

▶ Use the closest setting possible if you do not have access to a bench with a 75° incline setting.

START

FINISH

THE SET UP

TRAINER TIPS

1. Pick up the dumbbells using a neutral grip and sit on the bench with them resting on your thighs, close to your hip crease.

2. Position your feet shoulder-width apart, under or behind your knees and flat on the floor.

3. Lie back, using your thighs to help get the dumbbells into position level with your chest.

4. Hold the dumbbells directly above your elbows, with your upper arms at an angle of 45-60° to your torso.

5. Point your chest up towards the ceiling and pinch your shoulder blades back together.

6. Your shoulders and glutes should be touching the bench, and there will be a small gap between your lower back and the bench.

7. This is the start and finish position for each rep.

- Do not place your feet on top of the bench. Keep them flat on the floor.

- Be very careful when manoeuvring the dumbbells in and out of position. Getting set-up to dumbbell press can be an awkward process with heavy weights, which is why we typically stick to using more moderate weights and higher reps on this exercise.

THE MOVEMENT

TRAINER TIPS

1. Press both dumbbells directly upwards until you have fully extended your arms overhead.

2. Reverse the motion, under control, to return to the start position.

3. You have reached the end of your range-of-motion when you cannot lower your elbows any further below shoulder height without your chest collapsing and shoulders rotating inwards.

4. Pause for a moment before repeating for the desired number of reps.

5. On the last rep, lower the dumbbells to the start position, tuck your elbows in and sit forwards using your legs to help generate momentum. Alternatively, your training partner can help by taking one dumbbell from you at a time.

- The set-up and movement are the same as other versions of the dumbbell bench press but this angle places more emphasis on your shoulders.

- The dumbbells should not clang together at the top position.

- A common mistake is for your shoulders to become loose and shrug upwards at the top of the movement. This reduces stability and shifts tension away from your chest and onto your shoulders and triceps. Focus on pushing yourself away from the dumbbells, instead of pressing them away from you.

- Be careful not to push your head back into the bench, as this can strain your neck.

CHEST
CABLE FLY
(SEATED & STANDING)

Target Muscle Groups

Primary

· Chest (pectoralis major)

Secondary

· Shoulders (anterior deltoid)
· Arms (biceps brachii)

WHAT YOU NEED:

1. Cable crossover station.

2. Handle cable attachments.

3. Adjustable bench with a 75° incline setting.

NOTES:

▶ Use the closest setting possible if you do not have access to a bench with a 75° incline setting.

START

STANDING

FINISH

STANDING

THE SET UP

1. Adjust the cables to shoulder height when standing or seated.

i. For the seated version, position the bench in the middle of the cables and pulled forwards so that the back legs are one to two feet in front of the cables.

ii. Pick up the handles and sit on the bench. Point your chest up towards the ceiling and pinch your shoulder blades back together.

iii. For the standing version, pick up the handles, stand in the middle of the cables and take a long stride forward. Adopt a split-stance position with one foot in front of the other and bend forward slightly from the waist.

2. Bring your arms forwards so that they are at shoulder height and roughly in line with your armpits.

3. Hold the handles with a neutral grip and keep your elbows slightly bent.

4. This is the start and finish position for each rep.

TRAINER TIPS

▶ The cable crossover station is a popular piece of equipment, and it may be difficult to perform the seated version in a busy gym.

▶ Choose one version, seated or standing, and perform it consistently for an entire phase to avoid interrupting your progress.

THE MOVEMENT

1. Pull your arms forwards in a semi-circular motion, driving your upper arms into the sides of your chest.

2. Pause for a moment and focus on contracting (squeezing) your chest muscles.

3. Reverse the motion, under control, to return to the start position.

4. Repeat for the desired number of reps.

TRAINER TIPS

▶ The goal of the exercise is not to touch your hands together. They may or may not touch depending on the length of your forearm and the degree of elbow bend.

▶ Do not allow your elbows to travel behind your armpits, as this places an unwanted strain on your shoulders.

CHEST
DUMBBELL FLY

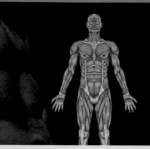

Target Muscle Groups

Primary

- Chest (pectoralis major)

Secondary

- Shoulders (anterior deltoid)
- Arms (biceps brachii)

WHAT YOU NEED:

1. Flat bench.

2. Pair of dumbbells.

NOTES:

▶ The bench should be wide enough to support your upper back and not so tall that you cannot keep your feet flat on the floor. Use an elevated surface, e.g. weight plates, to provide a stable base if you cannot keep your feet flat on the floor.

START

FINISH

THE SET UP

1. Pick up the dumbbells using a neutral grip and sit on the bench with the dumbbells resting on your thighs, close to your hip crease.

2. Position your feet shoulder-width apart, under or behind your knees and flat on the floor.

3. Lie back, using your thighs to help get the dumbbells into position level with your chest.

4. Point your chest up towards the ceiling and pinch your shoulder blades back together.

5. Your head, shoulders and glutes should be touching the bench, and there will be a small gap between your lower back and the bench.

6. Press both dumbbells upwards until you have fully extended your arms overhead.

7. Adopt a neutral grip and place a slight bend in your elbows, which you will keep fixed throughout the movement.

8. This is the start and finish position for each rep.

TRAINER TIPS ★

▶ Do not place your feet on top of the bench. Keep them flat on the floor.

▶ Even though you will be lifting relatively light weights compared to the dumbbell and barbell bench press, it is still important to go through the same detailed set-up procedure to get the most out of this exercise.

THE MOVEMENT

1. Lower both dumbbells out to your sides in a wide arc.

2. Pause for a moment before reversing the motion, under control, to return to the start position. Focus on driving your upper arms into the sides of your chest.

3. Repeat for the desired number of reps.

TRAINER TIPS

▶ Stop the upwards movement when the dumbbells are directly above your shoulders to keep tension on your chest muscles.

▶ Do not allow your elbows to travel below your armpits, as this places an unwanted strain on your shoulders.

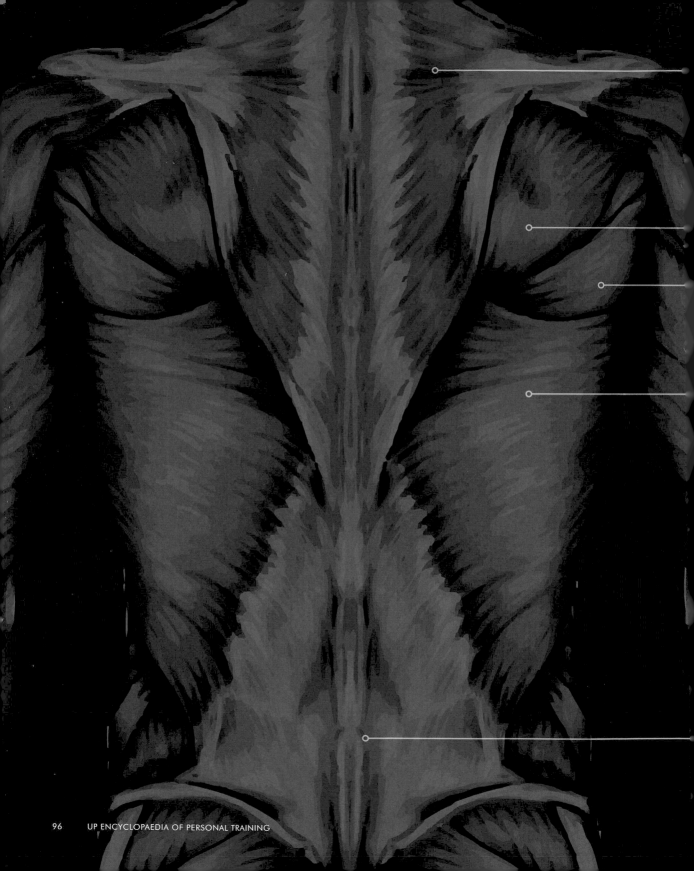

Trapezius

THE EXERCISE GUIDE

Rhomboid

Teres major

Latissimus dorsi

CABLE ROW *(NEUTRAL & OVERHAND GRIP)*

SINGLE ARM DUMBBELL ROW

CABLE PULL-DOWN *(NEUTRAL & OVERHAND GRIP)*

STRAIGHT ARM CABLE PULL-DOWN *(STANDING & CHEST SUPPORTED)*

CHEST SUPPORTED DUMBBELL ROW

Erector spinae

EXERCISE GUIDE

BACK
CABLE ROW
(NEUTRAL & OVERHAND GRIP)

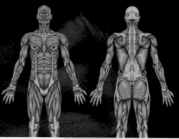

Target Muscle Groups

Primary

- Upper back (latissimus dorsi, rhomboids, trapezius and teres major)

Secondary

- Shoulders (posterior deltoid)
- Arms (biceps brachii & brachialis)
- Forearms (brachioradialis)

WHAT YOU NEED:

1. Seated cable row station.
2. Shoulder-width neutral grip cable attachment.
3. Shoulder-width overhand grip cable attachment.
4. Weightlifting straps.

NOTES:

▶ There are several different versions of the cable row machine. Some will have a seat, possibly even with a chest support, while in other versions you sit on the floor.

▶ Avoid using cable attachments that are narrower than shoulder-width, as they restrict your range-of-motion during the movement.

▶ Make sure to use weight lifting straps to stop your grip strength from limiting how much weight you can lift and forearm fatigue distracting you during a set.

START — NEUTRAL GRIP

OVERHAND GRIP

FINISH — NEUTRAL GRIP

OVERHAND GRIP

THE SET UP

1. Sit on the machine (or floor) facing the weight stack with your feet on the foot supports (or base of the machine), and knees slightly bent.

2. Reach forward and grip the cable attachment with either a neutral or overhand shoulder-width grip.

3. Sit up as tall as possible with your arms fully extended reaching out in front of you.

4. This is the start and finish position for each rep.

TRAINER TIPS

▶ Choose one version, neutral grip or overhand grip, and perform it consistently for an entire phase to avoid interrupting your progress.

THE MOVEMENT

1. Keeping your torso still, pull your elbows back towards your waist while squeezing your shoulder blades together.

2. Keep your elbows tucked in so that your upper arms brush against your sides throughout the movement.

3. You have reached the end of your range-of-motion when your elbows cannot travel any further back without your shoulders rotating inwards and upper back rounding.

4. Pause for a moment and focus on contracting (squeezing) your upper back muscles.

5. Reverse the motion, under control, to return to the start position.

6. Repeat for the desired number of reps.

TRAINER TIPS

▶ Avoid pulling the cable attachment too high towards your chest as this will shift tension off your upper back muscles and onto your arm muscles. Instead, focus on pulling your elbows towards your waist.

▶ Your arm muscles will be working, but you should not feel that they are doing more work than your upper back muscles.

▶ Watch how high the weight-stack travels on each rep as a reference point for your range-of-motion. If this shortens significantly between your first and last rep, then the weight is too heavy.

BACK
SINGLE ARM DUMBBELL ROW

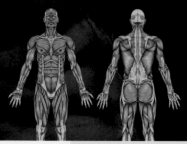

Target Muscle Groups

Primary

- Upper back (latissimus dorsi, rhomboids, trapezius and teres major)

Secondary

- Shoulders (posterior deltoid)
- Arms (biceps brachii & brachialis)
- Forearms (brachioradialis)

WHAT YOU NEED:

1. Flat bench.

2. Pair of dumbbells.

3. Weightlifting straps.

NOTES:

▶ Make sure to use weight lifting straps to stop your grip strength from limiting how much weight you can lift and forearm fatigue distracting you during a set.

START

FINISH

THE SET UP

1. Select your dumbbells and place one on each side of a flat bench.

2. Place the knee of your non-working side on the bench and your opposite foot a comfortable distance out to the side.

3. Align your knees so that your hips are straight and not twisted.

4. Lean forward until your torso is roughly parallel to the floor and use your non-working arm to support yourself.

5. Spread your bodyweight evenly across all three points of contact (hand, knee and foot).

6. Look at the floor just in front of you.

7. Pick up the dumbbell with your free hand and let your arm hang by your side, with your palm facing inwards.

8. This is the start and finish position for each rep.

TRAINER TIPS

▶ Placing your supporting hand too close to your body will cause you to hunch over, but too far away will strain your shoulder.

▶ Start with your weaker arm first and perform the same number of reps on both sides.

THE MOVEMENT

1. Keeping your torso still, pull your elbow and shoulder blade back towards your waist.

2. Keep your elbow tucked in so that your upper arm brushes against your side throughout the movement.

3. You have reached the end of your range-of-motion when your elbow cannot travel any further back without your shoulder rotating inwards and upper back rounding. Your elbow should not move past the front of your shoulder.

4. Pause for a moment and focus on contracting (squeezing) your upper back muscles.

5. Reverse the motion, under control, to return to the start position.

6. Repeat for the desired number of reps and then switch sides.

TRAINER TIPS

▶ Take 30 to 60 seconds extra rest when changing sides to let any tiredness in your supporting arm pass.

▶ Keep your back straight and do not allow your torso to rotate on the upwards movement, as this reduces your range-of-motion.

▶ Avoid pulling the dumbbell towards your shoulder as this will shift tension off your upper back muscles and onto your arm muscles. Instead, focus on dragging the dumbbell along the floor and pulling your elbow towards your waist.

▶ Your arms will be working, but you should not feel that they are doing more work than your upper back muscles.

EXERCISE GUIDE

BACK
CABLE PULL-DOWN
(NEUTRAL & OVERHAND GRIP)

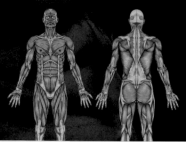

Target Muscle Groups

Primary

- Upper back (latissimus dorsi, rhomboids, trapezius and teres major)

Secondary

- Shoulders (posterior deltoid)
- Arms (biceps brachii & brachialis)
- Forearms (brachioradialis)

WHAT YOU NEED:

1. Pull-down station.

2. Shoulder-width neutral grip cable attachment.

3. Shoulder-width overhand grip cable attachment.

4. Weightlifting straps.

NOTES:

▶ Avoid using cable attachments that are narrower than shoulder-width, as they restrict your range-of-motion during the movement.

▶ Make sure to use weight lifting straps to stop your grip strength from limiting how much weight you can lift and forearm fatigue distracting you during a set.

START | NEUTRAL GRIP

OVERHAND GRIP

FINISH | NEUTRAL GRIP

OVERHAND GRIP

THE SET UP

1. Grip the cable attachment with either a neutral or overhand shoulder-width grip and sit down on the bench with your upper thighs securely positioned under the padding.

2. Sit up as tall as possible with your arms fully extended above your head, but avoid shrugging your shoulders up by your ears.

3. This is the start and finish position for each rep.

TRAINER TIPS

▶ Choose one version, neutral grip or overhand grip, and perform it consistently for an entire phase to avoid interrupting your progress.

▶ Adjust the thigh pads so that when you are in position there is no gap between your upper thighs and the pad.

▶ Do not lean back more than one to two inches, as this changes the emphasis of the exercise turning it into more of a row-like movement than a pull-down.

THE MOVEMENT

1. Keeping your torso still, pull your elbows down towards your waist while squeezing your shoulder blades back together.

2. You have reached the end of your range-of-motion when your elbows cannot travel any further without your shoulders rotating inwards and upper back rounding.

3. Pause for a moment and focus on contracting (squeezing) your upper back muscles.

4. Reverse the motion, under control, to return to the start position.

5. Repeat for the desired number of reps.

TRAINER TIPS

▶ Watch how high the weight-stack travels on each rep as a reference point for your range-of-motion. If this shortens significantly between your first and last rep, then the weight is too heavy.

▶ Although your arm muscles contribute to the movement, this exercise primarily targets your upper back muscles. Think of your arms as hooks that connect to the weight and are pulled down by your back muscles.

BACK
STRAIGHT ARM CABLE PULL-DOWN
(STANDING & CHEST SUPPORTED)

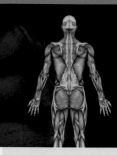

Target Muscle Groups

Primary

- Upper back (latissimus dorsi, rhomboids, trapezius and teres major)

Secondary

- Shoulders (posterior deltoid)
- Arms (triceps brachii)

WHAT YOU NEED:

1. Cable pulley station.

2. Two standard length rope attachments.

3. Adjustable bench with a 45° incline setting.

NOTES:

▶ Make sure the ropes are not twisted, or they will be slightly different lengths.

▶ Performing this exercise with your chest supported on a bench will help you to maintain a stable torso position and to focus on the movement.

▶ Secure the bench with something heavy to keep it securely in place.

▶ Use the closest setting possible if you do not have access to a bench with a 45° incline setting.

START

CHEST SUPPORTED

FINISH

CHEST SUPPORTED

THE SET UP

1. Adjust the cable to the highest setting and attach two standard length rope attachments.

i. If performing the standing version, hold the ropes with a neutral grip and take three to four steps back from the station. Position your feet shoulder-width apart, push your hips back and bend forward at the waist so that your torso is at a 45° angle to the floor.

ii. If performing the chest supported version, position the bench three to four steps back from the cable station, grip the attachment and lie face down on the bench. Press your hips into the bench and raise your chest up slightly.

2. Fully extend your arms out in front of you with your elbows slightly bent. Move further back if you cannot do this without the weights hitting the stack.

3. This is the start and finish position for each rep.

TRAINER TIPS

▶ Choose one version, chest supported or standing, and perform it consistently for an entire phase to avoid interrupting your progress.

THE MOVEMENT

1. Keeping your torso still, pull your elbows down towards your waist while squeezing your shoulder blades back together.

2. You have reached the end of your range-of-motion when your elbows cannot move any further back without your upper back rounding and shoulders rotating inwards.

3. Pause for a moment and focus on contracting (squeezing) your upper back muscles.

4. Reverse the motion, under control, to return to the start position.

5. Repeat for the desired number of reps.

TRAINER TIPS

▶ A common mistake is extending your elbows (like a cable triceps extension) to help finish the movement. The slight bend in your elbows should stay the same throughout the movement.

BACK
CHEST
SUPPORTED
DUMBBELL ROW

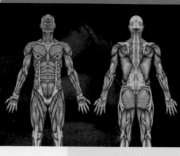

Target Muscle Groups

Primary

· Upper back (latissimus dorsi, rhomboids, trapezius and teres major)

Secondary

· Shoulders (posterior deltoid)
· Arms (biceps brachii & brachialis)
· Forearms (brachioradialis)

WHAT YOU NEED:

1. Adjustable bench with a 30º Incline setting.

2. Pair of dumbbells.

3. Weightlifting straps.

NOTES:

▶ Use the closest setting possible if you do not have access to a bench with a 30º incline setting.

▶ Make sure to use weight lifting straps to stop your grip strength from limiting how much weight you can lift and forearm fatigue distracting you during a set.

START

FINISH

THE SET UP

1. Select your dumbbells and place them on the floor at the head of the bench.

2. Lie face down on the bench, making sure that your chin clears the top edge.

3. Bend your legs and drive your feet into the floor.

4. Pick up the dumbbells one at a time and let your arms hang fully extended by your sides, with your palms facing inwards.

5. Press your hips into the bench, lift your chest up slightly and look at the floor just in front of you.

6. This is the start and finish position for each rep.

TRAINER TIPS

▶ Place your feet on the foot of the bench to help make yourself more stable. If the bench design does not allow for this, try using weight plates or heavy dumbbells as foot supports instead.

▶ Getting heavy dumbbells into position can be awkward, especially for people with short arms! Ask your training partner to pass you the dumbbells one at a time.

THE MOVEMENT

1. Pull your elbows back towards your waist while squeezing your shoulder blades together.

2. Keep your elbows tucked in so that your upper arms brush against your sides throughout the movement.

3. You have reached the end of your range-of-motion when your elbows cannot travel any further back without your shoulders rotating inwards and upper back rounding. Your elbows should not move past the front of your shoulders.

4. Pause for a moment and focus on contracting (squeezing) your upper back muscles.

5. Reverse the motion, under control, to return to the start position.

6. Repeat for the desired number of reps.

TRAINER TIPS

▶ Avoid pulling the dumbbells towards your shoulders as this will shift tension off your upper back muscles and onto your arm muscles. Instead, focus on dragging the dumbbells along the floor and pulling your elbows towards your waist.

▶ Your arm muscles will be working, but you should not feel that they are doing more work than your upper back muscles.

▶ If the pressure on your chest is too uncomfortable then select an alternative exercise.

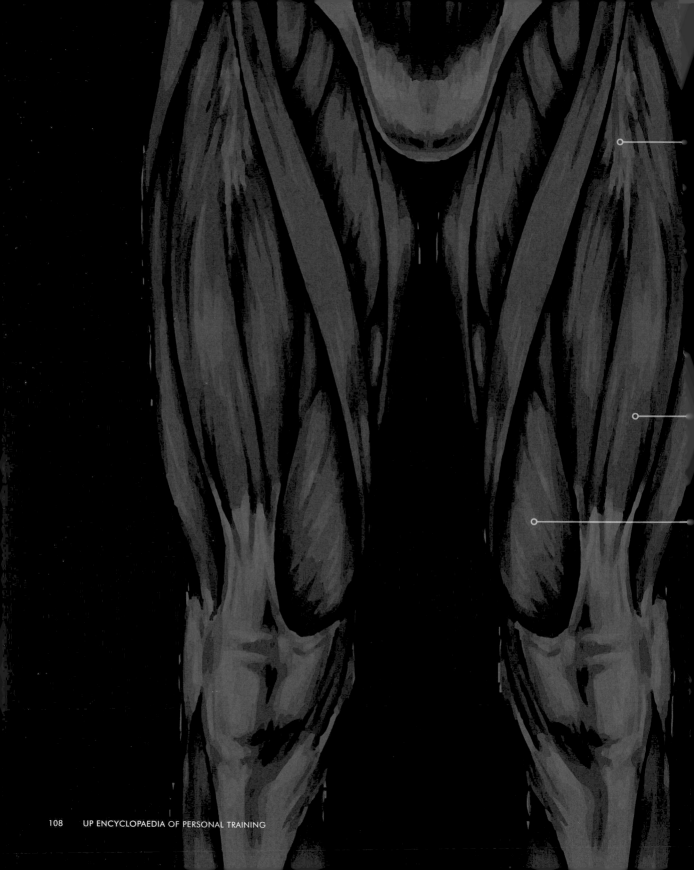

Rectus femoris

Vastus lateralis

Vastus intermedius

Vastus medialis

THE EXERCISE GUIDE

QUADRICEPS

45° INCLINE LEG PRESS

HORIZONTAL LEG PRESS

LEG EXTENSION

SPLIT SQUAT

SPLIT SQUAT *(FRONT & REAR FOOT ELEVATED)*

STEP-UP

QUADRICEPS
45° INCLINE LEG PRESS

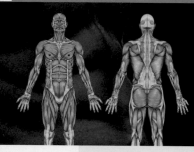

Target Muscle Groups

Primary

- Quadriceps muscle group
- Glutes (gluteus maximus)

Secondary

- Inner thigh (adductor muscle group)
- Calves (gastrocnemius and soleus)

WHAT YOU NEED:

1. 45° incline leg press machine.
2. Weight plates ranging from 1.25kg to 20kg.

NOTES:

▶ Most 45° incline leg press machines are plate loaded, which means that you need to add weight plates. In contrast, most horizontal leg press machines come pre-loaded with weight-stacks.

START

FINISH

THE SET UP

1. Load the weight plates onto the machine and set the safety stop in the right position for your range-of-motion.

2. Adjust the back pad so that it forms a 45-60° angle to the floor.

3. Sit down on the machine and place your feet on the platform shoulder-width apart.

4. Position your feet at a level that is comfortable for your ankles and allows you to push through the centre of your feet.

5. Grip the handles firmly and pull yourself down into the seat.

6. Straighten your legs to take the weight off the racks. On some machines, this will automatically unlock the safety mechanism, but on others, you will have to manually release it (instructions should be printed on the machine).

7. Your knees should be slightly bent.

8. This is the start and finish position for each rep.

TRAINER TIPS

▶ The safety stop allows you to limit the exercise range-of-motion. Start by performing a set with no added weight to test your range-of-motion without the pressure of heavy weights forcing you into compromising positions. Ideally, you will be able to set the safety stop precisely at the end of your range-of-motion, but the machine may not be a perfect match. In this case, select the closest setting within your range-of-motion.

▶ The weight you can lift on a plate loaded 45° incline leg press is not comparable to other leg press machines like the horizontal leg press.

THE MOVEMENT

1. Start the movement by lowering your legs to bring your knees in towards your chest.

2. You have reached the end of your range-of-motion when you cannot lower your legs any further without your heels lifting off the platform and buttocks lifting out of the seat.

3. Pause for a moment in the bottom position keeping tension in your legs.

4. Press both legs into the platform to return to the start position. Focus on pushing through the centre of your feet.

5. Repeat for the desired number of reps. On the last rep, make sure to re-engage the safety mechanism.

TRAINER TIPS

▶ Keep your knees in line with your feet and do not 'lock-out' your knees at any point.

▶ Only pause briefly in the top position between reps instead of resting for several seconds.

QUADRICEPS
HORIZONTAL LEG PRESS

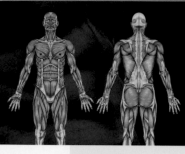

Target Muscle Groups

Primary

· Quadriceps muscle group
· Glutes (gluteus maximus)

Secondary

· Inner thigh (adductor muscle group)
· Calves (gastrocnemius and soleus)

WHAT YOU NEED:

1. Horizontal leg press machine.

NOTES:

▶ Most horizontal leg press machines are weight-stack machines, which means that the weight is pre-loaded onto the machine and you use the metal pin to select the weight you want to lift.

START

FINISH

THE SET UP

1. Adjust the back pad so that it forms a 45-60° angle to the floor.

2. Sit down on the machine and place your feet on the platform shoulder-width apart.

3. Adjust the proximity of the seat to the platform so that there is a roughly 90° bend in your knees.

4. Position your feet at a level that is comfortable for your ankles and allows you to push through the centre of your feet.

5. Grip the handles firmly and pull yourself down into the seat.

6. Press against the platform to create tension in your legs.

7. This is the start and finish position for each rep.

TRAINER TIPS

▶ The weight you can lift on a horizontal leg press machine is not comparable to other leg press machines including the 45° Incline Leg Press.

THE MOVEMENT

1. Start the movement by pressing through both legs to push yourself away from the platform.

2. Focus on pushing through the centre of your feet and stop just short of fully straightening your legs.

3. Reverse the motion, under control, to return to the start position.

4. Pause for a moment in the bottom position keeping tension in your legs.

5. Repeat for the desired number of reps.

TRAINER TIPS

▶ Keep your knees in line with your toes and do not 'lock-out' your knees at any point.

▶ Only pause briefly in the top position between reps instead of resting for several seconds.

QUADRICEPS
LEG
EXTENSION

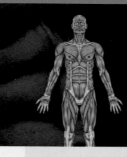

Target Muscle Groups

Primary

· Quadriceps muscle group

WHAT YOU NEED:

1. Leg extension machine.

NOTES:

START

FINISH

THE SET UP

1. The first step is to adjust the machine settings to suit you:

i. Adjust the back-pad angle to a position somewhere between 75-90º.

ii. Sit down on the machine and place your shins behind the lower leg support pad. Pull yourself back into the seat so that the underside of your knees touch the edge of the seat.

iii. Adjust the seat (in or out) so that your knee joint lines up with the machine pivot point.

iv. Adjust the machine lever (up or down) so that your knees are bent at roughly 90º in the bottom position.

2. Sit upright, grip the handles and pull yourself down into the seat. Point your toes up toward the ceiling.

3. This is the start and finish position for each rep.

TRAINER TIPS

▶ Some machines are more adjustable than others. Follow the guidelines as closely as possible.

▶ If you have long femurs (thigh bones) and cannot adjust the machine set-up to align your knees with the machine pivot point, then select an alternative exercise to avoid straining your knees.

▶ If you have short femurs (thigh bones) and cannot adjust the machine set-up to align your knees with the machine pivot point, you can position yourself further forwards on the seat by placing a cushion or pad behind your back.

THE MOVEMENT

1. Extend your knees to straighten your legs.

2. Pause for a moment and focus on contracting (squeezing) your quadriceps muscles.

3. Reverse the motion, under control, to return to the start position.

4. Repeat for the desired number of reps.

TRAINER TIPS

▶ Grip the handles hard and keep pulling yourself down into the seat throughout the set, which will allow you to engage your quadriceps muscles more forcefully. Some machines even come equipped with seat belts to help keep you locked into position.

QUADRICEPS
SPLIT SQUAT

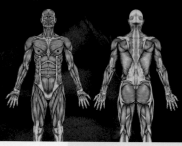

Target Muscle Groups

Primary

- Quadriceps muscle group
- Glutes (gluteus maximus)

Secondary

- Inner thigh (adductor muscle group)
- Calves (gastrocnemius and soleus)

WHAT YOU NEED:

1. Pair of dumbbells.

2. Non-slip flooring.

3. Weightlifting straps.

NOTES:

▶ Performing the exercise in front of a mirror can help with balance.

▶ Make sure to use weight lifting straps to stop your grip strength from limiting how much weight you can lift and forearm fatigue distracting you during a set.

START

FINISH

THE SET UP

1. Stand in an open space with your feet shoulder-width apart.

2. Place your hands on your hips and tuck your elbows in if you are performing bodyweight split squats. Alternatively, if using dumbbells, let them hang by your sides with your palms facing inwards.

3. Step forwards with your front leg and plant your foot flat on the floor.

4. Raise the heel of your back foot so that only your toes are touching the floor with shoelaces facing down. Both your hips and back heel should be straight.

5. This is the start and finish position for each rep.

TRAINER TIPS

▶ Make sure you can perform the step-up with proper technique before progressing to this exercise.

▶ Start with bodyweight for resistance and only progress to using a dumbbell once you have completed the target number of reps and are happy with your technique. For more advice, refer to 'How to: Select the Right Weight'.

▶ Start with your weaker leg forwards first and perform the same number of reps on both sides.

▶ If your stride length is too short, then the heel of your front foot will lift in the bottom position. But, if it is too long you will feel an uncomfortable strain on the thigh of your back leg.

THE MOVEMENT

1. Drop your back knee down towards the floor and push your front knee forwards to close the gap between your hamstrings and calf.

2. In the bottom position, your front foot should be flat and your back knee bent at 90° and one to two inches above the floor.

3. Pause for a moment keeping your upper body braced and tension in your legs.

4. Push through both legs to reverse the motion and return to the start position.

5. Repeat for the desired number of reps and then switch sides.

TRAINER TIPS

▶ Take 30 to 60 seconds extra rest when changing sides to let any tiredness in your back leg pass.

▶ You can standardise the range-of-motion by placing a small block (one to two inches tall) below your back knee. Make contact, but do not rest, on each rep.

▶ Only pause briefly in the top position between reps instead of resting for several seconds.

QUADRICEPS
SPLIT SQUAT
(FRONT AND REAR FOOT ELEVATED)

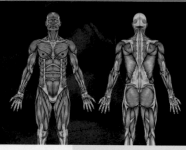

Target Muscle Groups

Primary

- Quadriceps muscle group
- Glutes (gluteus maximus)

Secondary

- Inner thigh (adductor muscle group)
- Calves (gastrocnemius and soleus)

WHAT YOU NEED:

1. Pair of dumbbells.

2. Non-slip flooring.

3. Raised platform approximately one to two inches above ankle height.

4. Weightlifting straps.

NOTES:

▶ Position a raised platform in an open space and secure it with something heavy or up against a wall to stop it sliding forwards.

▶ Performing the exercise in front of a mirror can help with balance.

▶ Make sure to use weight lifting straps to stop your grip strength from limiting how much weight you can lift and forearm fatigue distracting you during a set.

START

REAR FOOT ELEVATED

FINISH

REAR FOOT ELEVATED

THE SET UP

1. Stand with your feet shoulder-width apart and one stride length away from the platform, either facing towards (front foot elevated) or away from (rear foot elevated) the platform.
2. Place your hands on your hips and tuck your elbows in if you are performing bodyweight split squats. Alternatively, if using dumbbells, let them hang by your sides with your palms facing inwards.
3. If performing front foot elevated split squats, step forward with your front leg and plant your foot flat on top of the platform.
4. If performing rear foot elevated split squats, reach back with your back leg and place your foot on top of the platform.
5. Raise the heel of your back foot so that only your toes are touching the floor with shoelaces facing down. Both your hips and back heel should be straight.
6. This is the start and finish position for each rep.

TRAINER TIPS

▶ Make sure you can perform the step-up and front foot flat split squat with proper technique before progressing to this exercise.

▶ Start with bodyweight for resistance and only progress to using a dumbbell once you have completed the target number of reps and are happy with your technique. For more advice, refer to 'How to: Select the Right Weight'.

▶ Choose one version, front or rear foot elevated, and perform it consistently for an entire phase to avoid interrupting your progress.

▶ Start with your weaker leg forwards first and perform the same number of reps on both sides.

▶ If your stride length is too short, then the heel of your front foot will lift in the bottom position. But, if it is too long you will feel an uncomfortable strain on the thigh of your back leg.

THE MOVEMENT

1. Drop your back knee down towards the floor and push your front knee forwards to close the gap between your hamstrings and calf.
2. In the bottom position your front foot should be flat and your back knee bent at 90° and one to two inches above the floor.
3. Pause for a moment keeping your upper body braced and tension in your legs.
4. Push through both legs to reverse the motion and return to the start position.
5. Repeat for the desired number of reps and then switch sides.

TRAINER TIPS

▶ Take 30 to 60 seconds extra rest when changing sides to let the tiredness in your back leg pass.

▶ You can standardise the range-of-motion by placing a small block (one to two inches tall) below your back knee. Make contact, but do not rest, on each rep.

▶ Only pause briefly in the top position between reps instead of resting for several seconds.

▶ A common mistake when performing the front or rear foot elevated version of the split squat is not using the extra range-of-motion made possible by the raised platform. Your back knee should drop lower than on the flat foot version, but only if you can comfortably get into this position. If you cannot, then stick to the flat foot version.

EXERCISE GUIDE

QUADRICEPS
STEP-UP

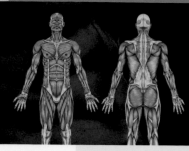

Target Muscle Groups

Primary

- Quadriceps muscle group
- Glutes (gluteus maximus)

Secondary

- Inner thigh (adductor muscle group)
- Calves (gastrocnemius and soleus)

WHAT YOU NEED:

1. Pair of dumbbells.

2. Adjustable step-up station or raised platform roughly one to two inches below knee height.

3. Weightlifting straps.

NOTES:

▶ Avoid using benches with softly cushioned upholstery to make sure that you can maintain a stable foot position.

▶ Make sure to use weight lifting straps to stop your grip strength from limiting how much weight you can lift and forearm fatigue distracting you during a set.

START

FINISH

THE SET UP

1. Stand facing the step-up platform with your feet shoulder-width apart.

2. Place your hands on your hips and tuck your elbows in if you are performing bodyweight step-ups. Alternatively, if using dumbbells, let them hang by your sides with your palms facing inwards.

3. Place the foot of your front leg on the platform in a position that allows you to push through the centre of your foot.

4. Make sure that your hips are straight and not twisted.

5. This is the start and finish position for each rep

TRAINER TIPS

▶ Start with bodyweight for resistance and only progress to using a dumbbell once you have completed the target number of reps and are happy with your technique. For more advice, refer to 'How to: Select the Right Weight'.

▶ Start with your weaker leg forwards first and perform the same number of reps on both sides.

THE MOVEMENT

1. Step up onto the platform using your front leg and resist the temptation to push up off your back leg.

2. Once you have fully straightened your front leg, bring your back leg forwards onto the platform.

3. Pause briefly and then step backwards with your back leg to return to the start position. Keep your front foot in position for the full set.

4. Repeat for the desired number of reps and then switch sides.

TRAINER TIPS

▶ Take 30 to 60 seconds extra rest when changing sides to let any tiredness pass.

▶ Only pause briefly in the top position between reps instead of resting for several seconds.

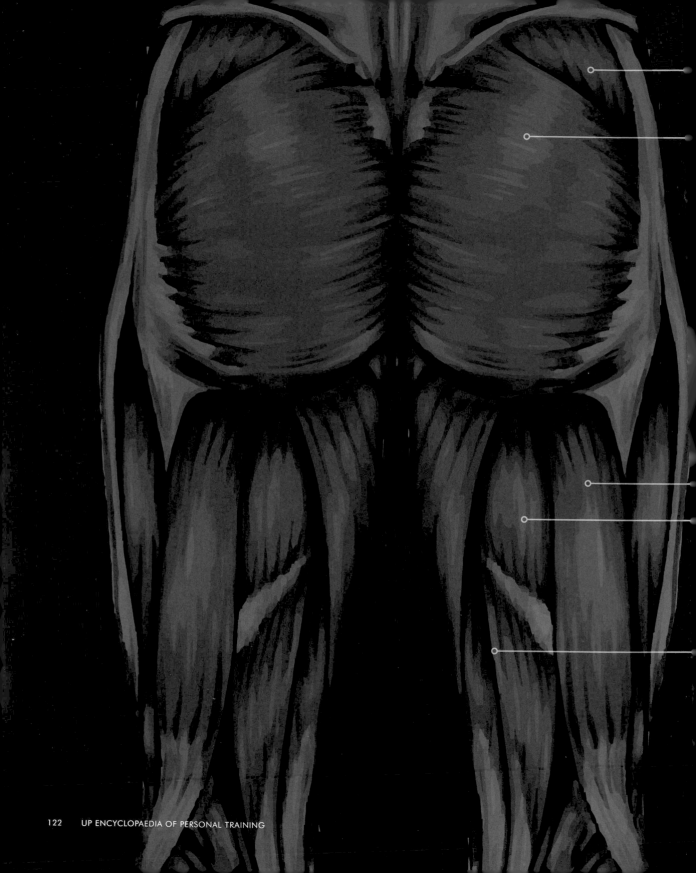

Gluteus medius

Gluteus maximus

THE EXERCISE GUIDE

GLUTES AND HAMSTRINGS

Biceps femoris

Semitendinosus

Semimembranosus

FLOOR GLUTE BRIDGE

HIP THRUST

BARBELL ROMANIAN DEADLIFT

INCLINE HIP EXTENSION *(45° INCLINE)*

WALKING LUNGE

REVERSE LUNGE

LEG CURL *(PRONE & SEATED)*

EXERCISE GUIDE

GETTING STARTED
HOW TO GET THE BARBELL INTO POSITION

WHAT YOU NEED:

1. Training partner.

2. Raised platform, e.g. wooden blocks or weight plates.

3. Bumper plates ranging from 5kg to 20kg.

THIS APPLIES TO THE FOLLOWING EXERCISES:

- Floor glute bridge
- Hip thrust

NOTES:

▶ When performing the floor glute bridge and hip thrust, unless you load two 20kg plates (typically the biggest plates) on each side of the barbell, you will struggle to roll the barbell up over your legs and into position over your hips.

▶ Bumper plates are a special type of weightlifting plate made from rubber. Unlike standard weightlifting plates, the different weight options are all the same diameter. As a result, you should have no problem getting the barbell into position no matter how much weight you are lifting.

HOW TO GET THE BARBELL INTO POSITION

START: Set the loaded barbell in position at your feet.

OPTION 1: If you are lifting at least 60kg (including the weight of the barbell) and using the larger sized 20kg plates, then you should be able to roll the barbell up over your legs and into position over your hips. This will also work if you are lifting less than 60kg, but have access to bumper plates.

OPTION 2: If you are lifting less than 60kg and do not have access to bumper plates, ask a training partner to lift the barbell in and out of position over your hips.

OPTION 3: The first approach is difficult for people with large legs, and the second option is dangerous with heavy weights. To avoid these problems either use bumper plates or position the barbell on a raised platform (e.g. wooden blocks or weight plates).

Following this, position the barbell in the crease of your hips and hold it in place with an overhand grip.

START

Start with loaded barbell in position at your feet.

OPTION 1

Barbell position if lifting at least 60kg.

OPTION 2

Getting barbell in position with a training partner.

OPTION 3

Getting barbell in position using a raised platform.

GLUTES & HAMSTRINGS
FLOOR GLUTE BRIDGE

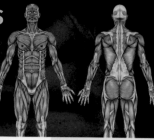

Target Muscle Groups

Primary
- Glutes (gluteus maximus)

Secondary
- Hamstrings muscle group
- Quadriceps muscle group
- Lower Back (erector spinae muscle group)

WHAT YOU NEED:

1. Exercise mat.
2. Dumbbell.
3. Barbell.
4. Barbell collars.
5. Weight plates ranging from 1.25kg to 20kg.
6. Bumper weight plates.
7. Cushioned bar pad.
8. Training partner.

NOTES:

▶ When you fit the barbell with the cushioned bar pad, make sure that the opening faces up, not down. Otherwise, it will slip off during the exercise.

START

FINISH

THE SET UP

1. Position an exercise floor mat in an open space and sit on the floor with your legs straight in front of you.

2. You can perform this exercise with bodyweight only, or you can use a single dumbbell or barbell for added resistance.

   Refer to page 124 for advice on how to get the barbell into position.

3. Lie back and tuck your feet in towards your buttocks. Keep your feet flat and roughly shoulder-width apart.

TRAINER TIPS

▶ Start with bodyweight for resistance and only progress to using free weights once you have completed the target number of reps and are happy with your technique. For more advice, refer to 'How to: Select the Right Weight'.

▶ With the correct foot position, your shins will be close to vertical at the top of the movement. Use the warm-up to experiment and find the position where you feel your glutes the most.

THE MOVEMENT

1. Drive your hips up towards the ceiling, pushing through your heels and squeezing your glutes. Keep your knees in line with your toes.

2. In the top position, your hips should be fully extended, and form a straight line between your upper back and knees.

3. Pause for a moment and focus on contracting (squeezing) your glutes.

4. Reverse the motion, under control, to return to the start position.

5. Repeat for the desired number of reps.

TRAINER TIPS

▶ Be careful not to overextend at the top of the movement by arching your lower back.

▶ Your lower back, hamstrings and quadriceps muscles will be engaged, but you should not feel that they are contributing more to the movement than your glutes.

GLUTES & HAMSTRINGS
HIP THRUST

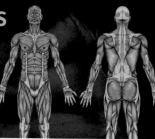

Target Muscle Groups

Primary

· Glutes (gluteus maximus)

Secondary

· Hamstrings muscle group
· Quadriceps muscle group
· Lower Back (erector spinae muscle group)

WHAT YOU NEED:

1. Flat bench.

2. Dumbbell.

3. Barbell.

4. Barbell collars.

5. Weight plates ranging from 1.25kg to 20kg.

6. Bumper weight plates.

7. Cushioned bar pad.

8. Training partner.

NOTES:

▶ When you fit the barbell with the cushioned bar pad, make sure that the opening faces up, not down. Otherwise, it will slip off during the exercise.

START

FINISH

THE SET UP

1. Position a flat bench in an open space and secure it with something heavy to prevent it sliding forwards.

2. Sit straight-legged on the floor with your upper back resting on the bench.

3. You can perform this exercise with bodyweight only, or you can use a single dumbbell or barbell for added resistance.

   Refer to page 124 for advice on how to get the barbell into position.

4. Tuck your feet in towards your buttocks. Keep your feet flat and roughly shoulder-width apart.

TRAINER TIPS

▶ Start with bodyweight for resistance and only progress to using free weights once you have completed the target number of reps and are happy with your technique. For more advice, refer to 'How to: Select the Right Weight'.

▶ With the correct foot position, your shins should be close to vertical at the top of the movement. Use the warm-up to experiment and find the position where you feel your glutes the most.

▶ A common mistake is not getting enough of your back on the bench, which increases the chances of sliding off! The bottom of your shoulder blades should be digging into the edge of the bench and will act as a pivot point during the movement.

THE MOVEMENT

1. Drive your hips up towards the ceiling, pushing through your heels and squeezing your glutes. Keep your knees in line with your toes.

2. In the top position, your hips should be fully extended, and your torso should be parallel to the floor.

3. Pause for a moment and focus on contracting (squeezing) your glutes.

4. Lower your hips down towards the floor. You have reached the end of your range-of-motion when you cannot move any further without your lower back rounding or knees rocking backwards.

5. Repeat for the desired number of reps.

TRAINER TIPS

▶ Be careful not to overextend at the top of the movement by arching your lower back.

▶ Your lower back, hamstrings and quadriceps muscles will be engaged but you should not feel that they are contributing more to the movement than your glutes.

▶ Avoid excessive movement of the head. Your neck should stay in line with your spine throughout the movement.

EXERCISE GUIDE

GLUTES & HAMSTRINGS

BARBELL ROMANIAN DEADLIFT

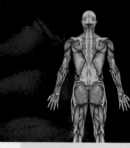

Target Muscle Groups

Primary

- Hamstrings muscle group
- Glutes (gluteus maximus)

Secondary

- Lower Back (erector spinae muscle group)
- Upper back (latissimus dorsi, rhomboids, trapezius and teres major)

WHAT YOU NEED:

1. Barbell.
2. Barbell collars.
3. Weight plates that range from 1.25kg to 20kg.
4. Weightlifting straps.
5. Power rack (optional).

NOTES:

▶ Make sure to use weight lifting straps to stop your grip strength from limiting how much weight you can lift and forearm fatigue distracting you during a set.

START

FINISH

THE SET UP

1. The first step is to get the barbell into position. If your gym has a power rack, set the hooks to hand-level when your arms are hanging by your side.

2. Place the barbell onto the hooks and add the desired amount of weight.

3. Stand close to the barbell with your feet shoulder-width apart and then reach down and grip the barbell with a shoulder-width overhand grip.

4. Lift the barbell off the hooks and take a step backwards.

5. Stand as tall as possible with your shoulder blades pulled back together and arms hanging by your sides. The barbell should be touching your thighs, and you should have a soft bend in your knees.

6. Look at the floor just in front of you.

7. This is the start and finish position for each rep.

TRAINER TIPS

▶ Make sure you can perform the incline hip extension with proper technique before progressing to this exercise.

▶ If your gym does not have a power rack, then use blocks to get the barbell as close to hand-level as possible. If this is not possible, you will have to deadlift the barbell from the floor.

THE MOVEMENT

1. Push your hips backwards and bend forward at the waist. The movement should come entirely from your hips, and you should feel a noticeable increase in hamstring tension.

2. Keep your back straight and pull the barbell into your body to stop it from drifting away from you.

3. You have reached the end of your range-of-motion when you cannot push your hips any further back without your lower back rounding or knees bending.

4. Pause for a moment in the bottom position and then drive your hips forwards and squeeze your glutes to return to the start position.

5. Repeat for the desired number of reps.

TRAINER TIPS

▶ Be careful not to overextend at the top of the movement by arching your lower back.

▶ Your lower back muscles will be engaged, but you should not feel that they are contributing more to the movement than your glutes and hamstrings.

EXERCISE GUIDE

GLUTES & HAMSTRINGS
INCLINE HIP EXTENSION
(45° INCLINE)

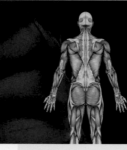

Target Muscle Groups

Primary

- Hamstrings muscle group
- Glutes (gluteus maximus)

Secondary

- Lower Back (erector spinae muscle group)
- Upper back (latissimus dorsi, rhomboids, trapezius and teres major)

WHAT YOU NEED:

1. 45° incline hip extension station.

2. Pair of dumbbells.

3. Weightlifting straps.

NOTES:

▶ Use dumbbells rather than a weight plate for added resistance. Weight plates typically increase in five to 10kg steps which are big increases when you measure it in relative (%) terms. For example, increasing from 5kg to 10kg is a 100% increase.

▶ Splitting the target weight across two dumbbells, e.g. 20kg = 2 x 10kg, is more comfortable than holding onto one heavier dumbbell.

START

FINISH

THE SET UP

1. If the station angle is adjustable, then set it to a 45° incline.

2. Climb onto the machine and lie face down with your ankles pressed firmly up against the foot pads.

3. If the thigh pad height is adjustable, then set it to cover your upper thighs. If the pad is too high, it will restrict your range-of-motion on the downward movement.

4. Squeeze your glutes to fully extend your hips so that your body makes a straight line with the angle of the station.

5. Cross your arms over your chest if using bodyweight for resistance. Alternatively, if using dumbbells let them hang below your shoulders with palms facing inwards.

6. Look at the floor just in front of you.

7. This is the start and finish position for each rep.

TRAINER TIPS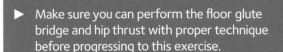

▶ Make sure you can perform the floor glute bridge and hip thrust with proper technique before progressing to this exercise.

▶ Start with bodyweight for resistance and only progress to using free weights once you have completed the target number of reps and are happy with your technique. For more advice, refer to 'How to: Select the Right Weight'.

▶ A common mistake is not leaning fully into the thigh pad for fear of falling. If you are worried about this, use the warm up to prove to yourself that the foot and thigh pads will hold you securely in place.

THE MOVEMENT

1. Push your hips backwards and bend forwards at the waist. The movement should come entirely from your hips and you should feel a noticeable increase in hamstring tension.

2. You have reached the end of your range-of-motion when you cannot push your hips any further back without your lower back rounding or knees bending.

3. Pause for a moment in the bottom position and then drive your hips forwards and squeeze your glutes to return to the start position.

4. Repeat for the desired number of reps.

TRAINER TIPS

▶ Be careful not to overextend at the top of the movement by arching your lower back.

▶ Your lower back muscles will be engaged, but you should not feel that they are contributing more to the movement than your glutes and hamstrings.

EXERCISE GUIDE

GLUTES & HAMSTRINGS
WALKING LUNGE

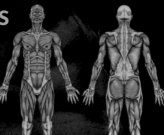

Target Muscle Groups

Primary

- Quadriceps muscle group
- Glutes (gluteus maximus)

Secondary

- Calves (gastrocnemius and soleus)
- Inner thigh (adductor muscle group)

WHAT YOU NEED:

1. Pair of dumbbells.

2. Non-slip flooring and open space to lunge into.

3. Weightlifting straps.

NOTES:

▶ Make sure to use weight lifting straps to stop your grip strength from limiting how much weight you can lift and forearm fatigue distracting you during a set.

START

FINISH

THE SET UP

1. Stand in an open space with your feet shoulder-width apart.
2. If performing bodyweight lunges, place your hands on your hips and tuck your elbows in. Alternatively, if using dumbbells, let them hang by your sides with your palms facing inwards.

TRAINER TIPS

▶ Start with bodyweight for resistance and only progress to using a dumbbell once you have completed the target number of reps and are happy with your technique. For more advice, refer to 'How to: Select the Right Weight'.

THE MOVEMENT

TRAINER TIPS

1. Take a long stride forward with your front leg and plant your foot firmly on the floor.
2. At the same time, raise the heel of your back foot so that only your toes are touching the floor with shoelaces facing down. Both your hips and the heel of your back foot should be straight.
3. Drop your back knee down towards the floor and push your front knee forwards to close the gap between your hamstrings and calf.
4. In the bottom position, your front foot should be flat and your back knee bent at 90° and one to two inches above the floor.
5. Pause for a moment keeping your upper body braced and tension in your legs.
6. Step forward onto your front leg and transition into the next rep by repeating the above steps with your back leg.
7. Repeat for the desired number of reps.

▶ If your stride length is too short, then the heel of your front foot will lift in the bottom position. But, if it is too long you will feel an uncomfortable strain on the thigh of your back leg.

▶ Make sure that you have securely planted your front foot before descending into the bottom position.

▶ If you struggle with balance, then try pausing for a second in the top position between reps.

▶ A common mistake is adopting too narrow of a stance. Think about standing on train tracks, not a tightrope.

EXERCISE GUIDE

GLUTES & HAMSTRINGS
REVERSE LUNGE

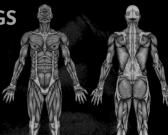

Target Muscle Groups

Primary

- Quadriceps muscle group
- Glutes (gluteus maximus)

Secondary

- Calves (gastrocnemius and soleus)
- Inner thigh (adductor muscle group)

WHAT YOU NEED:

1. Pair of dumbbells.

2. Non-slip flooring.

3. Weightlifting straps.

NOTES:

▶ Performing the exercise in front of a mirror can help with balance.

▶ Make sure to use weight lifting straps to stop your grip strength from limiting how much weight you can lift and forearm fatigue distracting you during a set.

START

FINISH

THE SET UP

1. Stand in an open space with your feet shoulder-width apart.

2. If performing bodyweight reverse lunges, place your hands on your hips and tuck your elbows in. Alternatively, if using dumbbells, let them hang by your sides with your palms facing inwards.

3. This is the start and finish position for each rep.

TRAINER TIPS

▶ Start with bodyweight for resistance and only progress to using a dumbbell once you have completed the target number of reps and are happy with your technique. For more advice, refer to 'How to: Select the Right Weight'.

THE MOVEMENT

1. Step backwards with your back leg and plant your foot on the floor with shoelaces facing down.

2. Drop your back knee down towards the floor and sink into the hip of your front leg.

3. In the bottom position, your front foot should be flat and back knee bent close to 90° and one to two inches above the floor.

4. Pause for a moment keeping your upper body braced and tension in your legs.

5. Step forward onto your front leg to return to the start position.

6. Repeat for the desired number of reps and then switch sides.

TRAINER TIPS

▶ Start with your weaker leg first and perform the same number of reps on both sides.

▶ Take 30 to 60 seconds extra rest when changing sides to let any tiredness in your back-leg pass.

▶ If your stride length is too short, then the heel of your front foot will lift in the bottom position. But, if it is too long you will feel an uncomfortable strain on the thigh of your back leg.

▶ Make sure that you have securely planted your back foot before descending into the bottom position.

▶ Only pause briefly in the top position between reps instead of resting for several seconds.

▶ You can standardise the range-of-motion by placing a small block (one to two inches tall) below your back knee. Make contact, but do not rest, on each rep.

EXERCISE GUIDE

GLUTES & HAMSTRINGS
LEG CURL
(PRONE & SEATED)

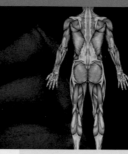

Target Muscle Groups

Primary
· Hamstrings muscle group

Secondary
· Calves (gastrocnemius and soleus)

WHAT YOU NEED:

1. Prone leg curl machine.

2. Seated leg curl machine.

NOTES:

▶ If your gym does not have a prone or seated leg curl machine, adapt the workout to include either the incline hip extension or barbell Romanian deadlift instead.

▶ If you do have to adapt the workout, make sure to pair both of these alternatives with an upper body pressing, rather than pulling exercise to avoid overlap in the muscle groups trained.

START

FINISH

THE SET UP

PRONE LEG CURL

1. Adjust the thigh pad to the incline setting.

i. Adjust the machine lever so that when you lie face down on the machine with your lower legs hooked underneath the ankle pad your knees are just short of full extension.

ii. Position yourself so that your knees line up with the machine pivot point.

2. Grip the handles, lift your chest up slightly, press your hips down into the pad and point your toes up towards your shins.

SEATED LEG CURL

1. Adjust the machine lever so that you can sit comfortably on the machine with your thighs underneath the lap pad and lower legs on top of the lower leg support pads.

i. Adjust the seat so that your knees line up with the machine pivot point.

ii. Adjust the lower leg support pads to a comfortable position just above your ankles.

iii. Adjust the lap pad to remove any gap between your thighs and the pad.

iv. Pull back on the machine lever to lift your legs up as high as is comfortable. You should feel a noticeable increase in hamstring tension but do not lock-out your knees.

v. Sit upright, grip the handles and pull yourself down into the seat. Point your toes up towards the ceiling.

THE MOVEMENT

PRONE LEG CURL

1. Push your thighs down into the pad and curl your legs up towards your buttocks.

2. You have reached the end of your range-of-motion when your knees are fully bent, or you cannot move any further without your hips or thighs lifting of the pad.

3. Pause for a moment and focus on contracting (squeezing) your hamstrings.

4. Reverse the motion, under control, to return to the start position.

5. Repeat for the desired number of reps.

SEATED LEG CURL

1. Curl your legs in towards your buttocks.

2. You have reached the end of your range-of-motion when your knees are fully bent, or you cannot move any further without arching your lower back.

3. Pause for a moment and focus on contracting (squeezing) your hamstrings.

4. Reverse the motion, under control, to return to the start position.

5. Repeat for the desired number of reps.

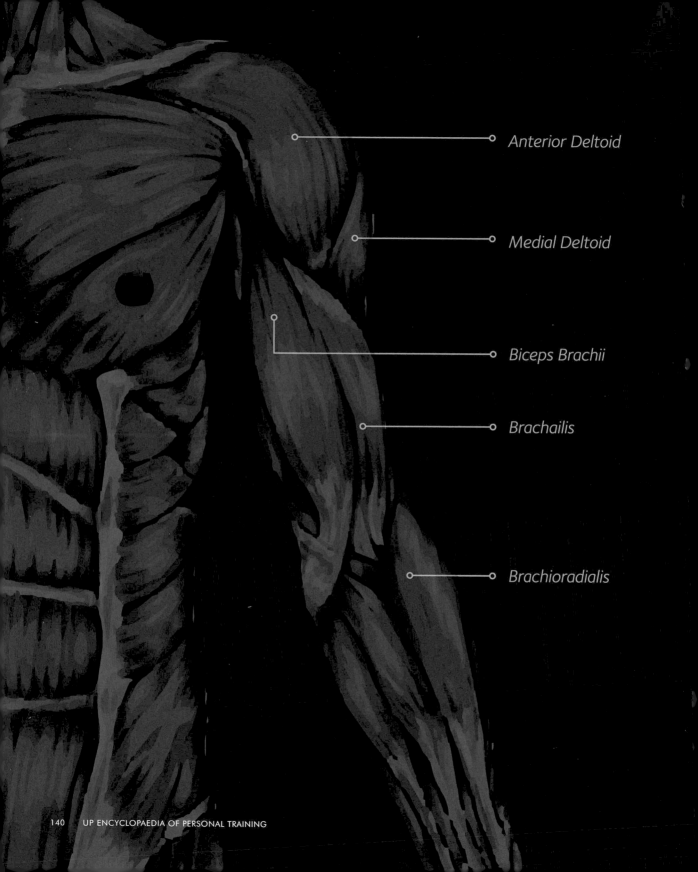

Anterior Deltoid

Medial Deltoid

Biceps Brachii

Brachailis

Brachioradialis

THE EXERCISE GUIDE

ARMS AND SHOULDERS

DUMBBELL BICEPS CURL *(UNDERHAND & NEUTRAL GRIP)*

DUMBBELL PREACHER CURL

SINGLE ARM PREACHER CURL *(DUMBBELL & CABLE)*

OVERHEAD CABLE TRICEPS EXTENSION

DUMBBELL TRICEPS EXTENSION

CABLE TRICEPS EXTENSION *(STANDING & KNEELING)*

DUMBBELL LATERAL RAISE *(SEATED & STANDING)*

SINGLE ARM CABLE LATERAL RAISE

EXERCISE GUIDE

ARMS AND SHOULDERS
DUMBBELL BICEPS CURL
(UNDERHAND & NEUTRAL GRIP)

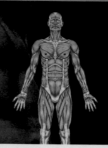

Target Muscle Groups

Primary

- Arms (biceps brachii and brachialis)

Secondary

- Forearms (brachioradialis)

WHAT YOU NEED:

1. Adjustable bench with an 80° Incline setting.

2. Pair of dumbbells.

NOTES:

▶ Use the closest setting possible if you do not have access to a bench with a 80° incline setting.

START | NEUTRAL GRIP

UNDERHAND GRIP

FINISH | NEUTRAL GRIP

UNDERHAND GRIP

THE SET UP

1. Pick up the dumbbells and sit on the bench.

2. Let your arms hang by your sides and hold the dumbbells with either an underhand or neutral grip.

3. Point your chest up and pinch your shoulder blades back together.

4. Position your elbows directly below your shoulders.

5. This is the start and finish position for each rep.

TRAINER TIPS

▶ Choose one version, neutral grip or underhand grip, and perform it consistently for an entire phase to avoid interrupting your progress.

THE MOVEMENT

1. Curl the dumbbells up towards your shoulders.

2. Keep your upper arms still and wrists straight throughout the movement.

3. You have reached the end of your range-of-motion when you cannot move any further without your shoulders or elbows pulling forwards.

4. Pause for a moment and focus on contracting (squeezing) your biceps.

5. Reverse the motion, under control, to return to the start position.

6. Repeat for the desired number of reps.

TRAINER TIPS

▶ Keep your upper arms still and elbows fixed below your shoulders to keep maximal tension on your biceps.

▶ Focus on curling your little finger up towards the ceiling to help create a more intense contraction.

▶ Single-joint exercises like the dumbbell biceps curl require less full body effort than multi-joint exercises, and it can be tempting to cut short your rest period. Make sure you stick to the recommended rest interval to give your muscles time to recover and maintain performance levels.

ARMS AND SHOULDERS
DUMBBELL PREACHER CURL

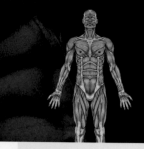

Target Muscle Groups

Primary

· Arms (biceps brachii and brachialis)

Secondary

· Forearms (brachioradialis)

WHAT YOU NEED:

1. Preacher curl bench.

2. Pair of dumbbells.

NOTES:

▶ If your gym does not have a preacher curl bench, you can perform the single-arm dumbbell version instead using an adjustable bench set to a 75° incline.

START

FINISH

THE SET UP

1. Sit down on the bench and rest your upper arms on the pad shoulder-width apart. The crease of your elbows should be facing up.

2. Adjust the pad or seat height so that your armpits line up with the top of the pad when seated. There should be no gap between your upper arms and the pad.

3. Hold the dumbbells with an underhand grip and with your elbows just short of full extension.

4. Keep your back straight and avoid hunching over the pad.

5. This is the start and finish position for each rep.

TRAINER TIPS

▶ Do not fully straighten your arms in the bottom position as this will place unwanted pressure on your elbows.

THE MOVEMENT

1. Press your upper arms down into the pad and curl the dumbbells up towards your shoulders.

2. Keep your wrists straight and palms facing up throughout the movement.

3. You have reached the end of your range-of-motion when you cannot move any further without lifting your elbows off the pad.

4. Pause for a moment and focus on contracting (squeezing) your biceps.

5. Reverse the motion, under control, to return to the start position.

6. Repeat for the desired number of reps.

TRAINER TIPS

▶ Focus on curling your little finger up towards the ceiling to help create a more intense contraction.

▶ Single-joint exercises like the preacher curl require less full body effort than multi-joint exercises, and it can be tempting to cut short your rest period. Make sure you stick to the recommended rest interval to give your muscles time to recover and maintain performance levels.

▶ Press your upper arms down into the pad throughout the entire movement.

EXERCISE GUIDE

ARMS AND SHOULDERS
SINGLE-ARM PREACHER CURL
(DUMBBELL & CABLE)

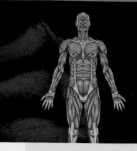

Target Muscle Groups

Primary

- Arms (biceps brachii and brachialis)

Secondary

- Forearms (brachioradialis)

WHAT YOU NEED:

1. Preacher curl bench.

2. Adjustable bench with a 75° incline setting.

3. Dumbbell.

4. Cable pulley station.

5. Handle cable attachment.

NOTES:

▶ If your gym does not have a preacher curl bench, you can perform the exercise standing using an adjustable bench set to a 75° incline instead, but you will have to use a dumbbell as the bench will block the cable's path.

START

CABLE

FINISH

CABLE

THE SET UP

1. If performing the cable version, adjust the cable to the lowest setting and position the bench three to four feet back from the station.

2. Sit down on the bench and rest your upper arm on the pad in line with your shoulder and with the crease of your elbow facing up.

3. Adjust the pad or seat height so that your armpit lines up with the top of the pad when seated. There should be no gap between your upper arm and the pad.

4. Hold the dumbbell or cable with an underhand grip and with your elbow just short of full extension.

5. Position your body so that your torso is pointing roughly 20-30° away from your arm.

6. Hold onto the bench with your other arm for support.

7. This is the start and finish position for each rep.

TRAINER TIPS

▶ Choose one version, dumbbell or cable, and perform it consistently for an entire phase to avoid interrupting your progress.

▶ Avoid pairing two unilateral (single-side) exercises together or as part of the same circuit. Unilateral exercises have several benefits, but including too many in all or a specific stage of your workout can take a long time to complete and interrupt your workout flow.

▶ Start with your weaker arm first and perform the same number of reps on both sides.

▶ Do not fully straighten your arm in the bottom position as this will place unwanted pressure on your elbow.

THE MOVEMENT

1. Press your upper arm down into the pad and curl the dumbbell or cable handle up towards your shoulder.

2. Keep your wrist straight and palm facing up throughout the movement.

3. You have reached the end of your range-of-motion when you cannot move any further without lifting your elbow off the pad.

4. Pause for a moment and focus on contracting (squeezing) your biceps.

5. Reverse the motion, under control, to return to the start position.

6. Repeat for the desired number of reps and then switch sides.

TRAINER TIPS

▶ Focus on curling your little finger up towards the ceiling to help create a more intense contraction.

▶ Single-joint exercises like the preacher curl require less full body effort than multi-joint exercises, and it can be tempting to cut short your rest period. Make sure you stick to the recommended rest interval to give your muscles time to recover and maintain performance levels.

▶ Press your upper arm down into the pad throughout the entire movement.

EXERCISE GUIDE

ARMS AND SHOULDERS
OVERHEAD CABLE TRICEPS EXTENSION

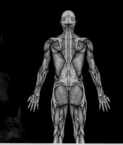

Target Muscle Groups

Primary

• Triceps (triceps brachii)

WHAT YOU NEED:

1. Cable pulley station.

2. Two standard length rope attachments.

3. Preacher curl bench.

NOTES:

▶ Using two standard length rope attachments will maximise your range-of-motion and allow you to extend your elbows fully.

▶ Make sure the ropes are not twisted, or they will be slightly different lengths.

START

FINISH

THE SET UP

1. Grip the rope attachments with a neutral grip and turn your body to face away from the weight stack, holding the ropes in place behind your neck.

2. Take a long stride forward and adopt a split-stance position with one foot in front of the other.

3. Push your hips back and bend forwards from the waist so that your torso is at a 45-60° angle to the floor.

4. Position your upper arms at shoulder-height and tuck your elbows in.

5. Tuck your chin in so that the rope does not hit your head during the movement.

6. This is the start and finish position for each rep.

TRAINER TIPS

▶ You can perform this exercise with your elbows supported on a preacher curl bench for improved stability. However, this may be difficult to do in a busy gym.

THE MOVEMENT

1. Keeping your upper arms and torso still, extend your elbows to straighten your arms.

2. You have reached the end of your range-of-motion when you cannot straighten your arms any further without your elbows flaring out and shoulders rotating inwards.

3. Pause for a moment and focus on contracting (squeezing) your triceps.

4. Reverse the motion, under control, to return to the start position.

5. Repeat for the desired number of reps.

TRAINER TIPS

▶ Make sure to move through the fullest range-of-motion possible, fully flexing your elbows on the return to the start position.

▶ Keep your upper arms still and do not let the weight pull you out of position. The only movement should come from your forearms hinging on your elbow joints.

▶ Single-joint exercises like the overhead cable triceps extension require less full body effort than multi-joint exercises, and it can be tempting to cut short your rest period. Make sure you stick to the recommended rest interval to give your muscles time to recover and maintain performance levels.

EXERCISE GUIDE

ARMS AND SHOULDERS
DUMBBELL TRICEPS EXTENSION

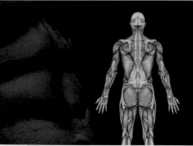

Target Muscle Groups

Primary

• Arms (triceps brachii)

WHAT YOU NEED:

1. Flat bench.

2. Pair of dumbbells.

NOTES:

▶ The bench should be wide enough to support your upper back and not so tall that you cannot keep your feet flat on the floor. Use an elevated surface, e.g. weight plates, to provide a stable base if you cannot keep your feet flat on the floor.

START

FINISH

THE SET UP

1. Pick up the dumbbells using a neutral grip and sit on the bench with them resting on your thighs, close to your hip crease.

2. Position your feet shoulder-width apart, under or behind your knees and flat on the floor.

3. Lie back, using your thighs to help get the dumbbells into position level with your chest.

4. Point your chest up towards the ceiling and pinch your shoulder blades back together.

5. Your head, shoulders and glutes should be touching the bench, and there will be a small gap between your lower back and the bench.

6. Using a neutral grip, press both dumbbells directly upwards until you have fully extended your arms overhead.

7. Tuck your elbows in and position your upper arms perpendicular to the floor.

8. This is the start and finish position for each rep.

TRAINER TIPS

▶ Even though you will be lifting relatively light weights compared to the dumbbell and barbell bench press, it is still important to go through the same detailed set-up procedure to get the most out of this exercise.

THE MOVEMENT

1. Keeping your upper arms still, bend your elbows to lower the dumbbells down towards your shoulders.

2. You have reached the end of your range-of-motion when you have fully flexed your elbows.

3. Pause for a moment before reversing the motion, under control, to return to the start position.

4. Repeat for the desired number of reps.

TRAINER TIPS

▶ Make sure to move through the fullest range-of-motion possible, fully flexing your elbows on the downwards movement.

▶ Keep your upper arms still and do not let the weight pull you out of position. The only movement should come from your forearms hinging on your elbow joints.

▶ Keep your elbows tucked in and do not let them flare out at any point during the movement.

▶ Single-joint exercises like the dumbbell triceps extension require less full body effort than multi-joint exercises, and it can be tempting to cut short your rest period. Make sure you stick to the recommended rest interval to give your muscles time to recover and maintain performance levels.

ARMS AND SHOULDERS
CABLE TRICEPS EXTENSION
(STANDING & KNEELING)

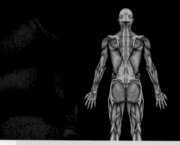

Target Muscle Groups

Primary

- Arms (triceps brachii)

WHAT YOU NEED:

1. Cable pulley station.

2. Two standard length rope attachments.

NOTES:

▶ Using two standard length rope attachments will maximise your range-of-motion and allow you to extend your elbows fully.

▶ Make sure the ropes are not twisted, or they will be slightly different lengths.

▶ Performing this exercise from a more stable kneeling position may help you to focus on the movement.

START

KNEELING

FINISH

KNEELING

THE SET UP

1. Adjust the cable to the highest setting and attach two standard length rope attachments.

2. Hold the ropes with a neutral grip and take three to four steps back from the station.

i. If performing the standing version, stand with your feet shoulder-width apart, push your hips back and lean forward slightly.

ii. If performing the kneeling version, kneel with your knees shoulder-width apart, push your hips back and lean forward slightly.

3. Squeeze your shoulder blades back together and pull your elbows back behind your shoulders.

4. This is the start and finish position for each rep.

▶ Choose one version, kneeling or standing, and perform it consistently for an entire phase to avoid interrupting your progress.

▶ When performing the standing version, to avoid the weight hitting the stack and limiting your range-of-motion, you will have to stand slightly further back and lean forwards more.

THE MOVEMENT

1. Keeping your upper arms and torso still, extend your elbows to straighten your arms.

2. You have reached the end of your range-of-motion when you cannot move any further without your upper back rounding and shoulders rotating inwards.

3. Pause for a moment and focus on contracting (squeezing) your triceps.

4. Reverse the motion, under control, to return to the start position.

5. Repeat for the desired number of reps.

▶ Make sure to move through the fullest range-of-motion possible, fully flexing your elbows on the return to the start position.

▶ Keep your upper arms still and do not let the weight pull you out of position. The only movement should come from your forearms hinging on your elbow joints.

▶ Single-joint exercises like the cable triceps extension require less full body effort than multi-joint exercises, and it can be tempting to cut short your rest period. Make sure you stick to the recommended rest interval to give your muscles time to recover and maintain performance levels.

ARMS AND SHOULDERS

DUMBBELL LATERAL RAISE
(SEATED & STANDING)

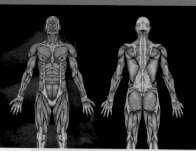

Target Muscle Groups

Primary
- Shoulders (medial deltoid)

Secondary
- Upper back (trapezius)

WHAT YOU NEED:

1. Adjustable bench with a 75° incline setting.
2. Pair of dumbbells.

NOTES:

▶ Performing this exercise with your chest supported on a bench will help you to maintain a stable torso position and to focus on the movement.

▶ If performing the standing version, secure the bench with something heavy to stop it from sliding forwards.

▶ Use the closest setting possible if you do not have access to a bench with a 75° incline setting.

START

STANDING

FINISH

STANDING

THE SET UP

1. If performing the seated version, pick up the dumbbells and sit at the end of a flat bench. Lean forward slightly from the waist and keep your back straight.

i. If performing the standing version, pick up the dumbbells, straddle the bench and lean into it so that your torso angle matches the bench angle.

2. Hold the dumbbells with a neutral grip and let your arms hang by your sides with a small bend in your elbows.

3. This is the start and finish position for each rep.

TRAINER TIPS

▶ Choose one version, seated or standing, and perform it consistently for an entire phase to avoid interrupting your progress.

▶ The lateral raise is a complex exercise and it can take several workouts to refine your technique. Make sure to start light and only increase the weight when you are happy with your technique.

THE MOVEMENT

1. Push the dumbbells out to your sides while keeping your shoulders depressed. Your elbows should travel just in front of your shoulders.

2. You have reached the end of your range-of-motion when you cannot lift the dumbbells any higher without your shoulders shrugging upwards.

3. Pause for a moment before reversing the motion, under control, to return to the start position.

4. Repeat for the desired number of reps.

TRAINER TIPS

▶ Keep your little finger slightly higher than your thumb throughout the movement to keep maximal tension on your medial deltoid.

▶ If you cannot pause briefly in the top position, then you have used momentum to complete the movement and may need to lower the weight.

▶ Single-joint exercises like the lateral raise require less full body effort than multi-joint exercises, and it can be tempting to cut short your rest period. Make sure you stick to the recommended rest interval to give your muscles time to recover and maintain performance levels.

ARMS AND SHOULDERS

SINGLE ARM CABLE LATERAL RAISE

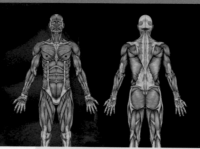

Target Muscle Groups

Primary

- Shoulders (medial deltoid)

Secondary

- Upper back (trapezius)

WHAT YOU NEED:

1. Cable pulley station.
2. Handle cable attachment.

NOTES:

▶ Some handle attachments can be awkward to hold and make it difficult to get into the correct set-up position. Look for a webbed handle attachment that allows you to adjust your grip or hold onto the cable directly by gripping the small ball.

START

FINISH

THE SET UP

1. Adjust the cable height to hand-level when your arms are hanging by your sides.

2. Stand side on and roughly one to two feet away from the cable pulley.

3. Reach across your body with your working arm and pick up the handle attachment.

4. Stand with your feet shoulder-width apart, lean forward slightly and hold onto the machine with your other arm for support.

5. Pull the hand of your working arm into position directly below your shoulder with your elbow slightly bent.

6. This is the start and finish position for each rep.

▶ Start with your weaker arm first and perform the same number of reps on both sides.

▶ The lateral raise is a complex exercise and it can take several workouts to refine your technique. Make sure to start light and only increase the weight when you are happy with your technique..

▶ Avoid pairing two unilateral (single-side) exercises together or as part of the same circuit. Unilateral exercises have several benefits, but including too many in all or a specific stage of your workout can take a long time to complete and interrupt your workout flow.

THE MOVEMENT

TRAINER TIPS

1. Push your hand out to your side while keeping your shoulder depressed. Your elbow should travel just in front of your shoulder.

2. You have reached the end of your range-of-motion when you cannot lift the cable any higher without your shoulder shrugging upwards.

3. Pause for a moment before reversing the motion, under control, to return to the start position.

4. Repeat for the desired number of reps and then switch sides.

▶ Keep your little finger slightly higher than your thumb throughout the movement to keep maximal tension on your medial deltoid.

▶ Single-joint exercises like the lateral raise require less full body effort than multi-joint exercises, and it can be tempting to cut short your rest period. Make sure you stick to the recommended rest interval to give your muscles time to recover and maintain performance levels.

▶ If you cannot pause briefly in the top position, then you have used momentum to complete the movement and may need to lower the weight.

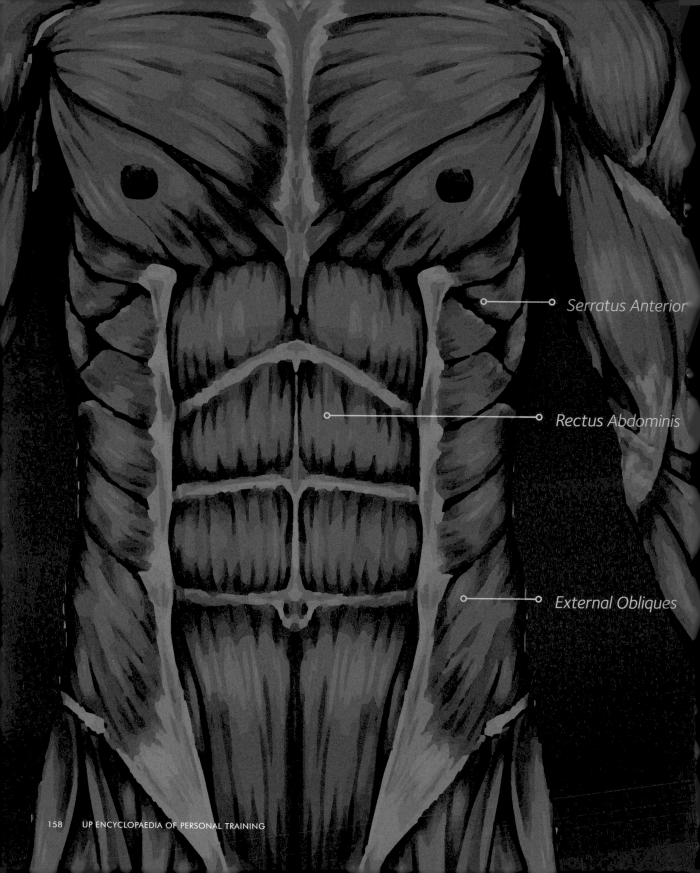

Serratus Anterior

Rectus Abdominis

External Obliques

THE EXERCISE GUIDE

ABDOMINALS

FLOOR CRUNCH

EXERCISE BALL CRUNCH

REVERSE CRUNCH *(FLAT & 20° INCLINE)*

ABDOMINALS
FLOOR CRUNCH

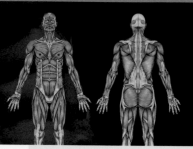

Target Muscle Groups

Primary

• Abdominals (rectus abdominis)

Secondary

• Abdominals
  (internal and external oblique)

WHAT YOU NEED:

1. Exercise mat.

2. Dumbbell.

NOTES:

▶ Use a dumbbell rather than a weight plate for added resistance. Weight plates typically increase in five to 10kg steps which are big increases when you measure it in relative (%) terms. For example, increasing from 5kg to 10kg is a 100% increase.

START

FINISH

THE SET UP

1. Lie face up on an exercise mat with your knees bent and feet planted flat on the floor. There should be a slight arch in your lower back.

2. Cross your arms over your chest if you are performing bodyweight crunches. Alternatively, if using a dumbbell, hold it in place with both hands across your upper chest.

TRAINER TIPS

▶ Start with bodyweight for resistance and only progress to using a dumbbell once you have completed the target number of reps and are happy with your technique.

▶ Ask your training partner to restrain your knees (pull against) or tuck your feet under a piece of equipment, which will help you to engage your abdominal muscles more forcefully.

▶ Do not place your hands behind your head, as this can lead to you pulling on and straining your neck.

THE MOVEMENT

1. Engage your abdominal muscles and curl your upper back up off the mat.

2. You have reached the end of your range-of-motion when you cannot move any further without flexing your hips and lifting your lower back up off the floor.

3. Pause for a moment and focus on contracting (squeezing) your abdominal muscles.

4. Reverse the motion, under control, to return to the start position.

5. Repeat for the desired number of reps.

TRAINER TIPS

▶ Do not sit all the way up, as this shifts tension off your abdominal muscles and onto your hip flexor muscles. To control your range-of-motion, focus on shortening the distance between your sternum (breastbone) and belly button.

EXERCISE GUIDE

ABDOMINALS
EXERCISE BALL CRUNCH

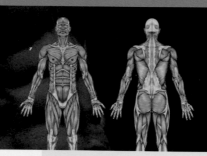

Target Muscle Groups

Primary

- Abdominals (rectus abdominis)

Secondary

- Abdominals
  (internal and external oblique)

WHAT YOU NEED:

1. Exercise ball.
2. Dumbbell.

NOTES:

▶ Exercise balls come in different sizes, and not every gym has every option available. Look for an exercise ball that allows you to keep your knees bent at roughly 90° in the set-up position.

▶ Use a dumbbell rather than a weight plate for added resistance. Weight plates typically increase in five to 10kg steps which are big increases when you measure it in relative (%) terms. For example, increasing from 5kg to 10kg is a 100% increase.

START

FINISH

THE SET UP

1. Select an appropriately sized exercise ball and sit on top of it in an open space.

2. Move forwards and slide down the exercise ball.

3. Stop when you find a comfortable position where the curvature of the ball matches the arch in your lower back.

4. Position your feet shoulder-width apart, under your knees and flat on the floor.

5. Cross your arms over your chest if you are performing bodyweight exercise ball crunches. Alternatively, if using a dumbbell, hold it in place with both hands across your upper chest.

TRAINER TIPS

▶ Make sure you can perform the floor crunch with proper technique before progressing to this exercise.

▶ Start with bodyweight for resistance and only progress to using a dumbbell once you have completed the target number of reps and are happy with your technique. For more advice, refer to 'How to: Select the Right Weight'.

▶ The exercise ball crunch is very similar to the floor crunch, but using an exercise ball allows you to move through a greater range-of-motion.

▶ Do not place your hands behind your head, as this can lead to you pulling on and straining your neck.

THE MOVEMENT

1. Engage your abdominal muscles and curl your upper back up off the exercise ball.

2. You have reached the end of your range-of-motion when you cannot move any further without flexing your hips and lifting your lower back up off the exercise ball.

3. Pause for a moment and focus on contracting (squeezing) your abdominal muscles.

4. Reverse the motion, under control, to return to the start position.

5. Repeat for the desired number of reps.

TRAINER TIPS

▶ Do not sit all the way up, as this shifts tension off your abdominal muscles and onto your hip flexor muscles. To control your range-of-motion, focus on shortening the distance between your sternum (breastbone) and belly button.

▶ Control your tempo on the downwards movement and only extend over the ball as far as is comfortable to avoid straining your back.

ABDOMINALS
REVERSE CRUNCH
(FLAT AND 20° INCLINE)

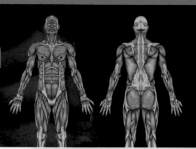

Target Muscle Groups

Primary

· Abdominals (rectus abdominis)

Secondary

· Abdominals
(internal and external oblique)

WHAT YOU NEED:

1. Adjustable bench with a flat and 20° Incline setting.

NOTES:

▶ Once you have completed the prescribed number of sets and reps using a flat bench, you can increase the challenge by setting the bench to a 20° incline, so that your head starts higher than your legs.

START

20° INCLINE

FINISH

20° INCLINE

THE SET UP

1. Lie face up on a flat bench with your knees tucked all the way in towards your chest.

2. Hold onto the head of the bench with both hands.

TRAINER TIPS

▶ Make sure you can perform the flat version with proper technique before progressing to the 20° incline version.

THE MOVEMENT

1. Engage your abdominal muscles and curl your lower back up off the bench.

2. You have reached the end of your range-of-motion when you cannot move any further without rolling up onto your upper back.

3. Pause for a moment and focus on contracting (squeezing) your abdominal muscles.

4. Reverse the motion, under control, to return to the start position.

5. Repeat for the desired number of reps.

TRAINER TIPS

▶ To control your range-of-motion, focus on shortening the distance between your belly button and sternum (breastbone).

▶ If you cannot feel an intense sensation in your abdominal muscles in the top position, then you are most likely using a combination of momentum and other muscles, e.g. hip flexors, to perform the movement.

EXTRAS

GLOSSARY

Body composition

The proportion of body fat and lean body mass (LBM) in your body. We generally express body composition in terms of body fat percentage, e.g. 10% body fat.

Bodyweight exercises

All exercises require you to lift a certain percentage of your bodyweight, but some are more demanding than others. For example, you lift your full bodyweight when performing split squats, but only the weight of your arms during a dumbbell curl.

Lifting your bodyweight can be challenging enough on some exercises to begin with and you do not need to add free weights.

Born-again beginner

Someone who has resistance training experience, but has not trained for an extended period due to competing demands on their time, injury or loss of motivation.

Cable machine

One of the three main types of resistance training machine. Cable machines consist of a weight-stack attached via a cable and pulley system to an attachment type of your choice.

Challenge set

A type of intensity technique that involves extending your set until you cannot complete another rep with proper technique.

Circuits

A type of exercise pairing, where you perform a series of exercises (more than two) in succession, separated by an appropriately sized rest period.

Complete beginner

Someone who has zero resistance training experience. Regardless of natural strength levels, build or sporting background, anyone engaging in resistance training for the first time is a complete beginner.

Concentric phase

The concentric phase is the part of a rep where your working muscles contract (shorten) while generating tension, which is known as a concentric muscle action.

De-training effect

The reversal of training adaptations (muscle hypertrophy, maximal strength and muscular endurance) towards pre-training levels in response to stopping training or significantly reducing your training volume.

Eccentric phase

The eccentric phase is the part of a rep where your working muscles lengthen while generating tension, which is known as an eccentric muscle action.

Energy expenditure

The amount of energy (calories) you expend carrying out a physical function. Your body expends energy maintaining basic life functions (e.g. breathing, blood circulation, etc.), digesting food and drink and when performing any movement from fidgeting to lifting weights.

Energy intake

The amount of energy (calories) you consume from food and drink.

Exercise order

The order you perform exercises in during a workout. We usually record exercise order in workout programs using letters, e.g. A, B, C, D, where each letter represents a different stage of the workout.

Exercise pairings

The different methods for grouping exercises. You can perform exercises one at a time (straight sets), paired together (paired sets), or as part of a longer sequence (circuits).

We usually record exercise pairings in workout programs using a combination of letters and numbers. For example, a single letter represents straight sets, e.g. A, and we pair letters and numbers together to represent paired sets, e.g. A1/A2, and circuits, e.g. A1/A2/A3.

Exercise selection

The exercises you choose to perform as part of your workout. There are several different exercises to choose from for each muscle group that differ in terms of complexity, biomechanical properties and equipment requirements.

Formal cardio

Structured cardio workouts deliberately performed as part of your training program.

Free weights

A form of resistance training equipment that is not attached to any machinery, such as pulleys or chains. The two main types are dumbbells and barbells, which unlike machines, give you complete control over the movement path.

Once you have mastered performing an exercise with just your bodyweight, you can use free weights to make it more challenging.

Full body workout

A type of workout design that includes at least one exercise for each of your major muscle groups (chest, back, quadriceps, glutes and hamstrings).

Functional beginner

Someone who has resistance training experience, but with limited success due to poor technique or training structure.

General warm-up

The first part of the recommended warm-up, which involves performing light physical activity, such as low to moderate intensity cardiovascular exercise.

High-intensity interval training (HIIT)

A type of formal cardio that alternates short periods of high-intensity exercise (RPE 7-10) with less intense recovery periods (RPE 2-3).

Hypertrophy

Hypertrophy describes the enlargement of an organ or tissue from an increase in the size of its constituent parts. The focus of this book is skeletal muscle hypertrophy, which is the scientific name for muscle building.

Informal cardio

All physical activity that is not planned exercise (resistance training or formal cardio). Typically referred to as NEAT (non-exercise activity thermogenesis), examples include walking to work, housework and even fidgeting!

Isometric phase

The isometric phase is the transition period between successive concentric and eccentric phases. During the isometric phase, your muscles are working, but there is no visible change in muscle length, which is known as an isometric muscle action.

Lean Body Mass (LBM)

A component of body composition, which you can calculate by subtracting your body fat weight from your total bodyweight. A common misunderstanding is that LBM only refers to muscle, when in fact it describes everything in your body apart from body fat. So, in addition to muscle, it also includes components such as organs, bones and skin.

Maximal strength

The maximum amount of force your muscles can produce during a single voluntary contraction. The combination of heavy weights and low reps are best for developing maximal strength.

You can test your maximal strength using a one-repetition max test, but this requires a high level of skill to achieve an accurate score and is not safe or practical to perform on every exercise. Alternatively, you can use one of several prediction equations (google 'Brzycki formula').

Moderate intensity steady state (MISS)

A type of formal cardio that involves performing moderate-intensity activity (RPE 5-6) for extended periods of time.

Multi-joint exercises

A type of exercise that involves movement at more than one joint and therefore trains several muscle groups at the same time (muscles pull on bones to create movement at a joint).

For example, the barbell bench press involves movement at both the shoulder and elbow joints and targets your chest, shoulder and triceps muscles.

Muscular endurance

The ability of your muscles to sustain repeated contractions against a resistance for an extended period. The combination of relatively light weights and high reps are best for developing muscular endurance.

GLOSSARY

Paired sets

A type of exercise pairing, where you perform two exercises in alternating fashion, separated by an appropriately sized rest period.

Periodisation

Planned variation in your workouts to optimise training outcomes and avoid plateaus. You can vary every component of your training program, including the number of sets and reps, type of exercise and training frequency. Making too many changes can be detrimental, but never changing your approach can lead to overuse injuries, strength plateaus, incomplete muscular development and boredom!

Plate-loaded machine

One of the three main types of resistance training machine. Unlike a weight-stack or cable machine, you must manually add weight plates onto the machine. The most common type of plate-loaded machine is the 45° incline leg press.

Primary muscle group

The muscle groups that are the major source of power during an exercise and should be what you feel working the most.

Range-of-motion (ROM)

A measure of the distance travelled during an exercise relative to the movement potential of the joints involved. You have reached the end of your ROM on an exercise when you cannot move any further without your technique failing.

Your ROM will shorten during a challenging set, as your muscles fatigue and cannot move the weights as far. Do not increase the weight used until ROM is the same for every rep. You can use the specific warm-up to determine your ROM for safe and effective training without the distraction of heavy weights.

Rate of perceived exertion (RPE) scale

A tool for measuring how hard you feel your body is working (perceived exertion) during physical activity. We use a version of an RPE scale to prescribe training intensity for the cardio program, as it is more practical than alternative methods, such as heart rate. The concept of RPE has traditionally been applied mostly to cardiovascular training, but new versions are being developed specifically for resistance training. We use a version

based on how close a set pushes you to failure to inform the weight selection process.

Relative strength

How strong you are for your size. The opposite of relative strength is absolute strength, which is the maximum amount of force you can produce, regardless of your body size.

Repetition (rep)

One complete motion of an exercise. We usually record reps in workout programs as a range, two reps wide, e.g. 8-10 reps.

The goal is to achieve the higher end of the range with your selected weight for all sets before increasing the weight used.

Repetition speed (tempo)

A measure of the speed you move at during a rep. We usually record rep speed in workout programs using a four-number sequence that prescribes a specific duration (in seconds) for the concentric, eccentric and isometric phases.

Repetitions in reserve (RIR)

How many extra reps you can perform (if any) at the end of a set. The accuracy of your estimates will increase over time, as you gain experience of performing different exercises and training close to failure.

Rest Day

A day during which no training sessions occur. You can have partial rest days where you do not resistance train but perform cardio, and complete rest days, where you do no formal training at all.

Rest periods

The time dedicated to recovery between sets and exercises. We usually record rest periods in workout programs as a range, e.g. 60-90 seconds. Make sure to rest for the lower limit, but you can start sooner than the upper limit if you feel ready.

Secondary muscle group

Muscle groups that play more of a supporting role during a movement, maintaining your posture and providing extra power to help the primary muscle groups.

Set

A specific number of reps of an exercise performed in succession.

Single-joint exercises

A type of exercise that involves movement at predominately one joint and therefore trains a more limited number of muscle groups compared to multi-joint exercises. For example, the dumbbell curl involves movement at the elbow joint and targets your arm muscles.

Specific warm-up

The second part of the recommended warm-up, which involves performing progressively heavier sets of the exercises you are going to be doing.

Straight sets

A type of exercise pairing, where you perform repeated sets of the same exercise, separated by an appropriately sized rest period.

Target areas

Body parts that you think are less well developed or want to focus more on compared to others.

Technical failure

The point in a set when your muscles are so fatigued that you cannot perform another rep with proper technique.

Technique

How you execute a movement. There is a general technical model for every exercise (outlined in the exercise guides), but how this looks in practice will vary slightly between individuals based on their body proportions.

Training age

An indicator of your training experience to date and potential for improvement moving forward. Beginners have very little (effective) training experience and huge potential for development, whereas advanced lifters have lots of experience and are much closer to their genetic upper limit.

Training frequency

How often you train a muscle group or exercise in a time-period, typically one week.

Training intensity

In the context of cardio, training intensity refers to how close to your maximum effort you reach when performing a bout of cardio.

In the context of resistance training, training intensity refers to how heavy a weight is relative to your maximum. The heavier the weight is, the more intense the exercise is.

Training volume

A measure of the total amount of mechanical work performed by your muscles during a set, workout, week, or some other measurement of training time. You can estimate training volume using the volume-load equation: total repetitions (sets x reps) x weight lifted.

We prescribe training volume in workout programs through training frequency, training intensity and the number of sets, reps and exercises.

Warm-up

All the activities that you perform in the period between walking onto the gym floor and starting the first set of your workout.

Weight-stack machine

One of the three main types of resistance training machine. With weight-stack machines, the weight is preloaded onto the machine, and you use a metal pin to select the weight you want to lift.

REFERENCES

INTRODUCTION

Bruusgaard, J., Johansen, I., Egner, I., Rana, Z. and Gundersen, K. (2010). Myonuclei acquired by overload exercise precede hypertrophy and are not lost on detraining. *Proceedings of the National Academy of Sciences*, 107(34), pp.15111-15116.

Correa, C., Baroni, B., Radaelli, R., Lanferdini, F., Cunha, G., Reischak-Oliveira, Á., Vaz, M. and Pinto, R. (2012). Effects of strength training and detraining on knee extensor strength, muscle volume and muscle quality in elderly women. *AGE*, 35(5), pp.1899-1904.

Fleck, S. and Kraemer W. (2014). '*Designing Resistance Training Programs*', 4th ed., Human Kinetics, pp. 179-212.

Helms, E., Aragon, A. and Fitschen, P. (2014). Evidence-based recommendations for natural bodybuilding contest preparation: nutrition and supplementation. *Journal of the International Society of Sports Nutrition*, 11(1), p.20.

Helms, E., Morgan, A. and Valdez, A. (2015). The Muscle and Strength Pyramid: Training. muscleandstrengthpyramids.com.

Katch, F., Katch, V., McArdle, W. (2014). '*Exercise Physiology: Nutrition, Energy, and Human Performance*', 8th ed., Lippincott Williams and Wilkins, pp. 500-538, 839-875.

Kraemer, W. and Hakkinen, K. (2001). '*Handbook of Sports Medicine and Science, Strength Training for Sport*', Blackwell Science Ltd, pp. 1-53.

GETTING STARTED

Helms, E., Fitschen, P., Aragon, A., Cronin, J. and Schoenfeld, B. (2015). Recommendations for natural bodybuilding contest preparation: resistance and cardiovascular training. *The Journal of Sports Medicine and Physical Fitness*, 55(3), pp.164-178.

Krieger, J. (2010). Single vs. Multiple Sets of Resistance Exercise for Muscle Hypertrophy: A Meta-Analysis. *Journal of Strength and Conditioning Research*, 24(4), pp.1150-1159.

Levine, J., Vander Weg, M., Hill, J. and Klesges, R. (2006). Non-Exercise Activity Thermogenesis: The Crouching Tiger Hidden Dragon of Societal Weight Gain. *Arteriosclerosis, Thrombosis, and Vascular Biology*, 26(4), pp.729-736.

MacDougall, J., Gibala, M., Tarnopolsky, M., MacDonald, J., Interisano, S. and Yarasheski, K. (1995). The Time Course for Elevated Muscle Protein Synthesis Following Heavy Resistance Exercise. *Canadian Journal of Applied Physiology*, 20(4), pp.481-485.

Nader, G. (2006). Concurrent Strength and Endurance Training: From Molecules to Man. *Medicine & Science in Sports & Exercise*, 38(11), pp.1965-1970.

Wernbom, M., Augustsson, J. and Thomee, R. (2007). The Influence of Frequency, Intensity, Volume and Mode of Strength Training on Whole Muscle Cross-Sectional Area in Humans. *Sports Medicine*, 37(3), pp.225-264.

Ralston, G., Kilgore, L., Wyatt, F. and Baker, J. (2017). The Effect of Weekly Set Volume on Strength Gain: A Meta-Analysis. *Sports Medicine*, pp.1-17.

Schoenfeld, B., Peterson, M., Ogborn, D., Contreras, B. and Sonmez, G. (2015). Effects of Low- vs. High-Load Resistance Training on Muscle Strength and Hypertrophy in Well-Trained Men. *Journal of Strength and Conditioning Research*, 29(10), pp.2954-2963.

Schoenfeld, B., Ratamess, N., Peterson, M., Contreras, B., Sonmez, G. and Alvar, B. (2014). Effects of Different Volume-Equated Resistance Training Loading Strategies on Muscular Adaptations in Well-Trained Men. *Journal of Strength and Conditioning Research*, 28(10), pp.2909-2918.

Wilson, J., Marin, P., Rhea, M., Wilson, S., Loenneke, J. and Anderson, J. (2012). Concurrent Training: A meta-analysis examining interference of aerobic and resistance exercises. *Journal of Strength and Conditioning Research*, 26(8), pp.2293-2307.

THE ANATOMY OF A WORKOUT

Benedict, T. (1999). Manipulating Resistance Training Program Variables to Optimize Maximum Strength in Men: A Review. *The Journal of Strength and Conditioning Research*, 13(3), pp.289-300.

Bird, S., Tarpenning, K. and Marino, F. (2005). Designing Resistance Training Programs to Enhance Muscular Fitness. *Sports Medicine*, 35(10), pp.841-851.

Campos, G., Luecke, T., Wendeln, H., Toma, K., Hagerman, F., Murray, T., Ragg, K., Ratamess, N., Kraemer, W. and Staron, R. (2002). Muscular adaptations in response to three different resistance-training regimens: specificity of repetition maximum training zones. *European Journal of Applied Physiology*, 88(1-2), pp.50-60.

REFERENCES

Chilibeck, P., Calder, A., Sale, D. and Webber, C. (1997). A comparison of strength and muscle mass increases during resistance training in young women. *European Journal of Applied Physiology*, 77(1-2), pp.170-175.

Fleck, S. and Kraemer W (2014). *'Designing Resistance Training Programs'*, 4th ed., Human Kinetics, pp. 1-61.

Hayes, L., Bickerstaff, G. and Baker, J. (2013). Acute Resistance Exercise Program Variables and Subsequent Hormonal Response. *Journal of Sports Medicine & Doping Studies*, 03(02), pp.1-7.

Kraemer, W. and Fragala, M. (2006). Personalize It. Program Design in Resistance Training. *ACSM's Health & Fitness Journal*, 10(4), pp.7-17.

Miranda, H., Fleck, S., Simão, R., Barreto, A., Dantas, E. and Novaes, J. (2007). Effect of Two Different Rest Period Lengths on the Number of Repetitions Performed During Resistance Training. *The Journal of Strength and Conditioning Research*, 21(4), pp.1032-1036.

Schoenfeld, B. (2010). The Mechanisms of Muscle Hypertrophy and Their Application to Resistance Training. *Journal of Strength and Conditioning Research*, 24(10), pp.2857-2872.

Schoenfeld, B. (2013). Is There a Minimum Intensity Threshold for Resistance Training-Induced Hypertrophic Adaptations?. *Sports Medicine*, 43(12), pp.1279-1288.

HOW TO TRAIN

Helms, E., Cronin, J., Storey, A. and Zourdos, M. (2016). Application of the Repetitions in Reserve-Based Rating of Perceived Exertion Scale for Resistance Training. *Strength and Conditioning Journal*, 38(4), pp.42-49.

McHugh, M. and Cosgrave, C. (2009). To stretch or not to stretch: the role of stretching in injury prevention and performance. *Scandinavian Journal of Medicine & Science in Sports*, 20(2), pp.169-181.

Shellock, F. and Prentice, W. (1985). Warming-Up and Stretching for Improved Physical Performance and Prevention of Sports-Related Injuries. *Sports Medicine*, 2(4), pp.267-278.

Zourdos, M., Klemp, A., Dolan, C., Quiles, J., Schau, K., Jo, E., Helms, E., Esgro, B., Duncan, S., Garcia Merino, S. and Blanco, R. (2016). Novel Resistance Training–Specific Rating of Perceived Exertion Scale Measuring Repetitions in Reserve. *Journal of Strength and Conditioning Research*, 30(1), pp.267-275.

ABOUT THE AUTHORS

ABOUT THE AUTHORS

NICK MITCHELL

Global CEO and Founder,
Ultimate Performance

Nick Mitchell is the founder of Ultimate Performance – the only global personal training business in the world, operating their own gyms across four different continents.

Hailed as 'one of the world's leading body composition experts' by multiple high profile publications, Nick is renowned for developing methodologies that have helped hundreds of thousands of people get in the best shape of their lives in the quickest possible time.

A multiple best-selling book author and a columnist in everything from Muscle & Fitness, Men's Health, Men's Fitness, Flex to the UK's Daily Telegraph, Nick spends what little spare time he has trying and failing to teach his children that daddy knows best.

JONATHAN TAYLOR

Deputy Head of Education
at Ultimate Performance

Principles of Muscle Building Program Design is Jonathan Taylor's first book, but it surely won't be his last.

Jonathan is the Deputy Head of Education at Ultimate Performance (UP) and is an instrumental part of the team that continues to cement UP's place at the top of the results producing tree across the global personal training industry.

A huge proponent of the benefits of hard work, Jonathan doesn't waste his time on social media but you can see multiple examples of his work on the UP twitter (@upfitness) and instagram pages (@upfitnesslive).

ACKNOWLEDGEMENTS

FROM NICK MITCHELL

The idea that we could write one all-encompassing book on the thought processes that go into how we do personal training at UP was often suggested to me, but was never going to fly in practice. What we do is simply far too complicated and involved.

Personal training is a very easy job to do, but a very difficult career to master.

That means that I came up with the idea for a series of books that has become the UP Encyclopaedia of Personal Training. As always, I tend to have the ideas and then I need to find someone brilliant, hard working, and in tune with my thoughts to get the job done. Step forward Jonathan Taylor, a man who deserves all the plaudits for the structure and incisive detail that makes this, our very first volume in the series, such a great read and fantastic resource. Everyone should watch Jonathan's progress, he's going to the stars.

I also want to give a secondary thanks to the entire personal training team at UP, especially Eddie Baruta and Sean Murphy. They work so hard to be the best at what they do and they make it easy for me and Jonathan to focus our attention on this book.

Last but by no means least, Andrew Cheung, UP's Head of Graphic Design, has to be thanked. No job is too small, no deadline is too tight. He works his socks off for the cause and if you enjoy this book then a large part of the credit should go to him.

FROM JONATHAN TAYLOR

I would like to take this opportunity to officially thank Nick Mitchell for the enormous impact he has had on my career to date.

Nick has not only created a business that has transformed thousands of client's lives, but also one that provides personal trainers like myself with an unrivalled environment to grow and develop in.

I also want to thank my parents, Michael and Linda Taylor, for their ongoing love and support. After proof-reading this book countless times, they now know more about resistance training than the average personal trainer!

Finally, I also owe huge thanks to Andrew Cheung for bringing this book to life, to Sean Murphy for his ongoing friendship and mentorship, and to all my clients past and present who I continue to learn from every day.